AROUND **denVer** WITH KIDS

by Christine Loomis

Fodor's Travel Publications
New York • Toronto • London • Sydney • Auckland

www.fodors.com

CREDITS
Writer: Christine Loomis

Series Editors: Karen Cure, Andrea Lehman
Editor: Matthew Lombardi
Editorial Production: Kristin Milavec
Production/Manufacturing: Yexenia (Jessie) Markland

Design: Fabrizo La Rocca, *creative director;*
Tigist Getachew, *art director*
Illustration and Series Design: Rico Lins, Keren Ora
Admoni/Rico Lins Studio

ABOUT THE WRITER

Christine Loomis is author of the Fodor's guide *Family Adventures* and former travel editor of *Parents* and *Family Life* magazines. A lifelong traveler, she has taken her three children exploring all over the world, but the place that remains closest to their hearts is their own home state of Colorado. Christine lives with her children and two well-traveled dogs in Boulder, Colorado.

FODOR'S AROUND DENVER WITH KIDS

Copyright © 2002 by Fodors LLC

Fodor's is a registered trademark of Random House, Inc. All rights reserved under International and Pan-American Copyright Conventions. Published in the United States by Fodor's Travel Publications, a unit of Fodors LLC, a subsidiary of Random House, Inc., and simultaneously in Canada by Random House of Canada Limited, Toronto. Distributed by Random House, Inc., New York.

ISBN 0-676-90187-5
ISSN 1537-5536
First Edition

IMPORTANT TIP

Although all prices, opening times, and other details in this book are based on information supplied to us at press time, changes occur all the time in the travel world, and Fodor's cannot accept responsibility for facts that become outdated or for inadvertent errors or omissions. So always confirm information when it matters, especially if you're making a detour to visit a specific place.

SPECIAL SALES

Fodor's Travel Publications are available at special discounts for bulk purchases for sales promotions or premiums. Special editions, including personalized covers, excerpts of existing guides, and corporate imprints, can be created in large quantities for special needs. For more information, contact your local bookseller or Special Markets, Fodor's Travel Publications, 280 Park Avenue, New York, NY 10017. Inquiries from Canada should be directed to your local Canadian bookseller or sent to Random House of Canada, Ltd., Marketing Dept., 2775 Matheson Boulevard East, Mississauga, Ontario L4W 4P7. Inquiries from the United Kingdom should be sent to Fodor's Travel Publications, 20 Vauxhall Bridge Road, London, England SW1V 2SA.

PRINTED IN THE UNITED STATES OF AMERICA
10 9 8 7 6 5 4 3 2 1

COUNTDOWN TO GOOD TIMES!

GET READY, GET SET!

Everyone knows that organizing a family's schedule is a full-time job. Pickups, drop-offs, school, parties, after-school activities—everyone off in a different direction. Of course, it's an organizer's dream, but a scheduling nightmare. Spending time together shouldn't be another thing to have to figure out.

We know what it's like to try to find good places to take your children or grandchildren. Sometimes it's tough to change plans when you suddenly hear about a kid-friendly event; besides, a lot of those events end up being crowded or, worse, sold out. It's also hard to remember places you read about in a newspaper or magazine, and sometimes just as hard to tell from the description what age group they're geared to. There's nothing like bringing a "grown-up" 12-year-old to an activity that's intended for his 6-year-old sister. Of course, if you're visiting Denver, it's even harder to figure out the best things to do with your kids before you even get there. That's where this book comes in.

You'll find here 68 ways to have a terrific couple of hours or an entire day with your children or your grandchildren. We've scoured the city, digging out activities your kids will love— from the eye-opening Black American West Museum to the state-of-the-art, high-tech USGS National Earthquake Information Center. The best part is that it's stress-free, uncomplicated, and easy for you. Open the book to any page and find a helpful description of a kid-friendly attraction, with age ratings to make sure it's right for your family, smart tips on visiting so that you can get the most out of your time there, and family-friendly eats nearby. The address, telephone number, open hours, and admission prices are all there for your convenience. We've done the work, so you don't have to.

Naturally you'll still want to keep an eye out for seasonal events that fit your family's interests. The National Western Stock Show and Rodeo in January is one of the biggest and best events of its kind in the country (don't forget to check out the champion bull that drinks from a silver bowl in the lobby of the historic Brown Palace Hotel). In February, Buffalo Bill's birthday is celebrated at the museum bearing his name, while the town of Golden celebrates Buffalo Bill Days in July with rides, games, and historic events. The Boulder Creek Festival in May is a not-to-be-missed event for all ages, and Denver's International BuskerFest, held in June on the Sixteenth Street Mall, takes visitors back to the days when some of the best entertainment was provided by jugglers and magicians on crowded street corners. In July the arts take center stage at the Cherry Creek Arts Festival and at the LoDo Music Festival, where young and old dance in the streets to all types of music. Fall brings another free outdoor celebration of the arts to Denver streets when the Colorado Performing Arts Festival showcases everything from cowboy poetry and storytelling to opera and classical ballet; in October, the Fort in Morrison is the scene of an authentic 1800s Encampment, complete with historical reenactors. There are lots of Halloween festivities to be found in the Denver metro area, from historic happenings at the Molly Brown House to the popular Boo at the Zoo, and many local farms offer pick-your-own pumpkins, hayrides, and children's mazes. Both the Sixteenth Street Mall and Larimer Square host a variety of family-oriented events throughout the year, and Denver shows off its ethnic diversity with Scottish, Irish, and Greek festivals, among others. To keep up with the latest happenings, go to www.denver.org/visitors and sign up for the free on-line newsletter from the Denver Convention and Visitors Bureau. That site also has a Kid's Stuff section, listing not only events and activities of interest to families, but also fun facts about Denver and Colorado and information for visitors with disabilities. The www.denvergov.org site lists all of Denver's attractions and provides links to their Web site for up-to-the-minute information on hours, new exhibits, expansions, and more. It's also the site for all kinds of transportation and visitor information—useful if you don't often navigate Denver's streets or public transportation system.

WAYS TO SAVE MONEY

We list only regular adult and kids' prices; children under the ages specified are free. It always pays to ask at the ticket booth whether any discounts are offered for a particular status or affiliation (but don't forget to bring your I.D.). Discounts are often available for senior citizens, AAA members, military personnel, and veterans, among others. Many attractions offer family memberships, generally good for one year of unlimited use for your family. These memberships sometimes allow you to bring a guest. Prices vary, but the memberships often pay for themselves if you visit the attraction several times a year. Sometimes there are other perks: newsletters or magazines, members-only previews, and discounts at a gift shop, for parking, or for birthday parties or special events. If you like a place when you visit, you can sometimes apply the value of your one-day admission to a membership if you do it before you leave. Keep in mind that many Denver attractions feature special free days during the year. The Denver Art Museum is free most Saturdays to Colorado residents, for example, and the Denver Zoo sometimes has half-price admission for visitors who arrive by Cultural Connection Trolley, so check for those deals on-line or call and ask. Denver's Scientific and Cultural Facilities District (SCFD), which underwrites some of the free days, also has its own Web site with lots of current information about events, activities, and attractions: www.artstozoo.org.

WHEN TO GO

With the exception of seasonal attractions, kid-oriented destinations are generally busiest when children are out of school—especially weekends, holidays, and summer—but not necessarily. Attractions that draw school trips can be swamped with clusters of children tall enough to block the view of your preschooler. But school groups tend to leave by early afternoon, so during the school year, weekdays after 2 can be an excellent time to visit museums, zoos, and aquariums. For outdoor attractions, it's good to visit after a rain, since crowds will likely have cleared out.

The hours we list are the basic hours, not necessarily those applicable on holidays. Some attractions are closed when schools are closed, but others add extra hours on these days. It's always best to check if you want to see an attraction on a holiday.

SAFETY

Obviously the amount of vigilance necessary will depend on the attraction and the ages of your kids. In crowded attractions, keep an eye on your children at all times, as their ages warrant. When you arrive, point out what the staff or security people are wearing, and find a very visible landmark to use as a meeting place, should you get separated. If you do split into groups, pick a time to meet. This will decrease waiting time, help you and your kids get the most out of your time there, and manage everyone's expectations.

FINAL THOUGHTS

Actually, this time it's yours, not ours. We'd love to hear what you or your kids thought about the attractions you visited. Or if you happened upon a place that you think warrants inclusion, by all means, send it along, so the next family can enjoy Denver even more. You can e-mail us at editors@fodors.com (specify the name of the book on the subject line), or write to Fodor's Around Denver with Kids, 280 Park Avenue, New York, NY 10017. We'll put your ideas to good use. In the meantime have fun!

—Christine Loomis

ADVENTURES OUT WEST

What better way to explore the sights around Colorado Springs than with experts who know the country, the history, the legends and lore, and some "secret" places you'd probably never find on your own? Adventures Out West (AOW) will put you in a commercial four-wheel-drive Jeep with roll bar, off-road tires, seating for six or seven (child carseats provided), and a suspension that can take just about anything. Behind the wheel, AOW's professional drivers, dressed in 1890s period clothing, take you scrambling through the canyons and into the foothills, all the while telling tall tales and true stories from Colorado's colorful past.

The combination of rugged driving and storytelling keeps most kids entertained, though with kids six and under, skip the full-day tours—even with interesting stops and stories, they require too much time strapped in a seat. One of the most dramatic tours is an early evening ride into the foothills overlooking Colorado Springs, entering Garden

HEY, KIDS! Bring along a copy of the lyrics for "America, the Beautiful" and take a look at it when you're up on Pikes Peak. It was the view from here, looking out over the city and plains and down to the San Juan Mountains, that inspired Katherine Lee Bates to write her poem in 1893. Especially on a nice, clear day, you can see what she meant when she talked about spacious skies, amber waves of grain, fruited plains, and purple mountains' majesty. Lots of people think "America, the Beautiful" should be our national anthem. What do you think?

of the Gods just as the massive red rock formations are lit by the setting sun. Three- to five-hour tours take you to North Cheyenne Canyon, Garden of the Gods, and Pikes Peak, past awesome waterfalls and old railroad beds, through tunnels, and into a historic district or two. Families with adolescents should consider the longer Cripple Creek Mining District trip, with a tour of the historic Molly Kathleen Mine (not for claustrophobics) included.

Tours cover a mix of paved roads, dirt roads, and 4X4 trails—you can specify whether you want a gentler or more rugged ride. AOW also organizes hiking trips (some with llamas) and combination Jeep/horseback trips; ask about adding photography lessons or entertainment. For groups of seven or more, AOW will pick you up in Denver (at additional cost), and they're considering Denver-based tours, so ask about that, too.

KEEP IN MIND
On tours that go into the mountains and foothills there's no access to public bathrooms until 30 to 60 minutes into the drive (depending on the destination), so make sure everyone in your group uses rest room facilities *before* getting into the Jeeps and heading out.

EATS FOR KIDS Bring your own snacks and food, arrange for Adventures Out West to provide lunches ($15 per person) with a tour, or go all out and order the Western barbecue ($25–$30, depending on menu). It's a definite plus for kids to have a barbecue with guys—and gals—dressed as cowpokes and serving up steak, chicken, and burgers with their six-shooters at their sides. Be sure to bring water, or order the cooler of beverages for the whole Jeep ($15).

When museum founder Paul W. Stewart was a child playing cowboys and Indians, he was told he couldn't be a cowboy because "there's no such thing as black cowboys." He was later to learn that nothing could be further from the truth: black men and women in fact played all kinds of significant roles in the development of the western United States. The Black American West Museum & Heritage Center, founded in 1971, preserves and displays artifacts from their lives, covering the period from the Civil War through World War II. Children enjoy becoming privy to this still-neglected part of American history, and adults—particularly if black history wasn't part of their curriculum in school—may also pick up on a thing or two.

The museum is located in the former home of Justina L. Ford, M.D., Colorado's first black female licensed physician. Ford was a medical pioneer who came to Denver in 1902 and,

KEEP IN MIND Five Points used to be a neighborhood with a reputation for being un-safe. Today it's a community on the rise, yet it remains one of Denver's authentic neighborhoods. There's no reason to feel uncomfortable either in and around the museum or at M&D Café.

HEY, KIDS! Did you know that nearly a third of all American cowboys were black? Some were good guys, others were way bad. Black cowboys rode with outlaws like Billy the Kid, Jesse James, the Daltons, and the Youngers. Most of these gangs have appeared in Hollywood movies, usually without mention of the black men who were a part of them. At the Black American West Museum you'll learn about lots of fascinating people, like tough guy Ferdinand Schavers, President Lincoln's personal bodyguard, and Henry Parker, a black mine owner who made one of the first discoveries of gold in Colorado.

3091 California St., Five Points

 $6 ages 13 and up,
$4.50 children 5–12

 303/296–2566; www.coax.net/
people/lwf/bawmus.htm

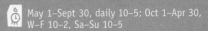 May 1–Sept 30, daily 10–5; Oct 1–Apr 30,
W–F 10–2, Sa–Su 10–5

5 and up

against great odds, earned a doctor's license. During her long practice she served people of varied ethnic backgrounds and all walks of life; her examining room is now one of the museum's permanent exhibits. The original museum collection was gathered personally by Paul Stewart as he traveled the West, meeting and talking with some of the black pioneers and cowboys whose stories the history books had ignored. From those first artifacts—legal documents, clothing, letters, photographs, and oral histories—the museum has grown to become one of the most comprehensive sources of historical material about African-Americans in the West. There are plenty of photographs and objects such as saddles, guns, and spurs to interest kids in the younger age range; there's also lots to read, and volunteers are adept at engaging kids with tales of real-life black gunslingers, lawmen, doctors, and miners.

EATS FOR KIDS **M&D Café** (2004 E. 28th St., tel. 303/296–1760), in the heart of Five Points, is a barbecue restaurant that's the real thing—a down-home, family-run joint with its own sauce and sweet-potato pie you've got to leave room for. It's a family-friendly place, and very popular; you may have to wait for seats at the old-fashioned Formica tables or stand in a long line for take-out, but if you're a barbecue lover, it's well worth your patience. There's plenty of fish if pork and beef aren't your thing. Warning: when they say hot, they mean *hot*.

BOULDER CREEK PATH

The wide, paved Boulder Creek Path runs for several miles along the creek and connects to many miles of the city's path system. Families on foot, bicycles, and skates enjoy the shade, the burbling creek, the surrounding green spaces, and the community activities that take place around the path. Near Fourth Street it becomes dirt and gravel and continues into the canyon—a route popular with cyclists and hikers.

To cool off, buy tubes at a gas station (about $10) and take a fun float (keep feet up to avoid rocks). At the west end of the creek you can watch kayakers on a white-water course, and on Wednesdays and Saturdays from April to October you can stroll through the popular farmers' market just east of Broadway (visit the Berry Best Smoothie cart for the top smoothies in town). The main branch of Boulder's Public Library, west of Broadway, has an excellent children's department and family-oriented programs. On the path between 28th and Folsom streets is an urban fish observatory where, standing on

EATS FOR KIDS The **Boulder Dushanbe Teahouse** (1770 13th St., tel. 303/442–4993; www.boulderteahouse.com), the only Persian teahouse in the Western Hemisphere, was handcrafted in Tajikistan as a gift for the people of Boulder "to make their souls happy." It achieves its goal with lavish, storybooklike motifs and furnishings. The eclectic menu includes chicken satay, plantain fritters, salads, teriyaki steak, rice pudding, and gingerbread ($4–$16); the children's menu has vegetarian, pasta, and chicken dishes, and weekend brunch plates (all $2.99). Kids can attend the Mad Hatter Children's Tea Party during the Rocky Mountain Tea Festival (July/Aug; tea sets available on-line).

 Parallel to Boulder Creek and
Arapahoe Ave., 55th St. to 4th St.

 303/442-2911 (Boulder Convention & Visitors
Bureau); www.bouldercoloradousa.com

 Free

 All hours

All ages

dry ground, you have a window onto the comings and goings of the creek's trout. Stop by Central Park, one of several creek-side parks, to see old engine #30, a monument to Boulder's railroading past; alas, climbing isn't allowed.

There are several annual festivals along the creek, including the Boulder Creek Festival on Memorial Day weekend, with rides, Native American art, kids' games, and food galore. Festivals are *always* crowded, so if you can take a backpack carrier rather than a stroller, do. There are several places to rent bikes; the Bikesmith (28th and Arapahoe, tel. 303/443–1132), has the kind for kids that attaches to a grown-up bike, for those who need extra pedal power. Come winter, take the path to the ice rink (near the Teahouse), where music mingles with the sound of rushing creek waters.

KEEP IN MIND
The creek is shallow in many places and people of all ages sit on the banks, wade, and dip their toes. But Boulder Creek can also be fast and deep; watch young children carefully, even if you're only down by the water for a minute.

HEY, KIDS! Boulder Creek has always been part of the city's history. In 1867 at what is now Broadway at the Creek, a 26-year-old horse thief was hanged by a mob. In 1894 a flood—predicted by an Arapaho warrior 36 years earlier—washed out every bridge from 4th Street to 17th Street. Although no one died, one fellow almost came to an untimely end at 9th Street when he fell into the raging water trying to save some chickens. It's said that Boulder is due for another "100-year flood"—but precautions have been taken to keep the city safe.

BOULDER OUTDOOR CENTER KAYAK CLINICS

Y ou won't find a more sports-oriented town than Boulder, or a better one in which to learn paddling and white-water skills. Taking a class with your kids is a way to open new doors in your relationship—and handing the teaching and rule-making over to someone else leaves you free simply to enjoy time together. Never mind that your kids will be impressed by how hip and cool Boulder Outdoor Center (BOC) instructors are; these folks know what they're doing, and most of them have spent many hours teaching families.

There are several class options depending on the season and the age of the children involved. For families with kids between 8 and 12 the best bet is a one-day lake clinic out at the Boulder Reservoir (the "Res") northeast of town. Although ages 8 and older are welcome to attend any of these scheduled clinics, keep in mind that they are seven hours long and have lots of information and instruction mixed in with the play. If you think your

HEY, KIDS!
Sign up on-line for BOCs sweepstakes—weekly in summer, bi-weekly in winter—to win paddles, booties, boats, snowshoes, and more. Enter by logging on to the center Web site, and remember you have to claim your prize within seven days.

EATS FOR KIDS There are two great delis not far from the Boulder Outdoor Center headquarters. **Salvaggio's** (2609 Pearl St., tel. 303/938–1981) is a traditional Italian deli with some of the best rotisserie prime rib sandwiches anywhere. **Deli Zone** (2900 Valmont, tel. 303/447–9349) is fashioned after a typical New York City delicatessen and serves up overstuffed sandwiches piled high with the deli meat of your choice. Whether or not you're a Big Apple aficionado, you're likely to go away happy. Note that lines can be long at both places.

 2510 47th St., Boulder

 303/444-8420;
www.boc123.com

 $34 (single class)–$359
(3-day clinic); ages 16 and
under receive a 50 percent
discount on some classes

 M–Sa 10–7

 8 and up

kids will have a hard time with instruction directed at a group, especially if the group is composed primarily of adults, consider private instruction. It's more expensive, but it's tailored to your family. If you have preteens (at least age 12) and teens, consider the three-day clinic, in which a day of building skills at the Res is followed by two days on local rivers. If your kids are intermediate or experienced paddlers, they can take part in clinics on rolling, surfing, and play-paddling—skills that give your adolescents the adrenaline rush they crave. All kids under 16 have to take classes with an adult, so here's your chance to challenge yourself and learn new skills, too.

Cold weather? Not to worry; BOC has clinics at area rec center indoor pools (frequently the Louisville center, east of Boulder). For many beginners, the comfortable confines of a heated pool are a good way to go, especially when learning rolling, which can be scary at first.

KEEP IN MIND Even in the heat of summer, the Boulder Reservoir has surprisingly chilly water, meaning you'll need a wetsuit (BOC supplies them) and you should bring warm clothes to pull on after class. If you're a family with one child too young to learn paddling, you can still spend the day together. One parent can take the clinic while the other hangs out with the younger child—lounging on the beach at the reservoir or playing in the rec center's slides and fountains. There are entrance fees at the reservoir and rec centers, both under $5 for adults.

BOULDER'S DINNER THEATRE

Some theaters accommodate children, while others truly welcome them. Boulder's Dinner Theatre (BDT) falls into the latter category. Producer Ross Haley writes in one of the theater's playbills, "we are ... delighted to have had so many young people in our audiences. We want live theatre to continue to grow through this new electronic age of computers, Internet, and television. Theatre will continue to thrive as young people experience the electricity and excitement that only live productions can generate." Kudos to Haley for putting on moderately priced, family-friendly shows (usually Broadway musicals; *My Fair Lady, Evita, Carousel,* and *42nd Street* have all been staged in recent years).

For any number of reasons, dinner theater is a particularly good choice for kids. First, they won't be hungry during the show, having just finished a full meal. And though dinner theater demands respect for both the actors and other viewers, it's a little less formal than traditional theater, so it's easier for families to relax and feel comfortable. The intimacy

KEEP IN MIND If you're tired of the same old venues for kids' birthday parties, here's an alternative that combines food and festivities while introducing children to first-class regional theater. Your group will get to see a play and meet the actors and actresses up close and personal as they're serving dinner. Not only that, the actors will acknowledge the event from the stage. Cake? No problem; Boulder's Dinner Theatre serves a very rich chocolate cake that's just right for the occasion. Call the main number for more information and to make arrangements.

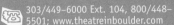

5501 Arapahoe Ave., Boulder

303/449-6000 Ext. 104, 800/448-5501; www.theatreinboulder.com

$35–$46.50, including dinner; $2 off for ages 12 and under T–Th and Su

T–Su 8 PM, Su matinee 2 PM

3 and up; higher suggested age for some shows

of the experience—there are 284 seats at tables for two, four, or six—plus the fact that the actors are the same people who have just served your meal, makes the show more accessible, and more fun, for kids. With the stage not far from any table, everyone can easily see the actors' expressions and hear the dialogue.

If there's a classic musical you loved as a child—or as an adult—it will probably make its way to BDT stage at some point, giving you and your kids the opportunity to tap toes together to a favorite song. Likewise, if there's a popular musical you've never gotten to see, this is a chance for the family to experience it together for the first time—all the while introducing your children to an art form that has entertained people for many centuries.

HEY, KIDS! Some musicals have found their inspiration in great books and even comic strips. *Oliver* was based on Charles Dickens's *Oliver Twist*. *Les Miserables*, by Victor Hugo, was turned into a Broadway hit. *Annie* came from a comic strip. Do you have a favorite book or comic that would make a good musical?

EATS FOR KIDS The ticket price includes the meal—salad, entrée, vegetable, and bread (but not drinks). There are generally chicken, beef, fish, and vegetarian dishes to choose from, and the menu always includes an item aimed at kids (ravioli, for example). Some entrées, such as prime rib and salmon, require an additional charge, and appetizers and desserts cost extra ($3.75–$6). Check out the ever-changing specialty show drinks (with or without alcohol), served in souvenir glasses the kids can take home (again for an extra charge).

BROWN PALACE AFTERNOON TEA

Tea at the Brown Palace Hotel isn't your typical mid-afternoon pick-me-up. It's an event, a very special (and correspondingly pricey) chance to be part of history. The hotel first opened its doors on August 12, 1892, and they've remained open every minute of every day since. Walk into the grand lobby and you're following in the footsteps of a slew of celebrities and U.S. presidents (including the Beatles and Dwight D. Eisenhower, both of whom have suites named after them).

Before or after tea, it's a must to visit the hotel's public rooms and take in some of its famous sights; ask at the front desk for a walking-tour pamphlet. Even younger kids will be impressed by the distinctive features of the Brown Palace, such as the 720-foot-deep well under the hotel that supplies all its water, and the annual January appearance in the lobby of a champion steer (who drinks water from a silver bowl) as part of the National

EATS FOR KIDS If you don't want to splurge on tea, eat downtown then tour the Brown Palace. **Crocodile Café** (1630 Market St., tel. 303/436–1144) has crayons for drawing and kids' dishes under $5. The main attraction is a 20-foot fake croc hanging from the ceiling.

HEY, KIDS! While waiting for tea to arrive (or oh-so-slow grown-ups to finish eating), look up at the six tiers of cast-iron balconies in the lobby atrium. Two of the hundreds of balcony panels, with their "dancing lady" design, were installed upside-down, making it look like the ladies are standing on their heads. Can you find them? Hint: they're on different sides of the room and different tiers. Still can't find them? Ask your server for more hints. Once you've succeeded, ask the adults with you to search—but don't give them too much help!

Western Stock Show. The pamphlet includes stories about some of the hotel artwork, explaining how it was created and who its subjects are.

The meal itself consists of a choice of teas served in delicate china pots plus tiny, sumptuous sandwiches, a variety of chocolates and other sweets, and traditional scones with decadent Devonshire cream (shipped from England, thank you) to slather on them—all arranged on dainty carousels at your table. (You can order salad, too, but that misses the point.) This is a great people-watching opportunity. The Brown Palace has been drawing socialite ladies in fancy hats, political bigwigs, cowboys, oil men, and regular folks from day one. Service remains impeccable. You just can't help feeling special as you perch on a plush sofa surrounded by onyx walls and pillars (12,400 square feet of onyx in all), sipping tea while a harpist plays in the background.

KEEP IN MIND While you don't have to dress up, it's fun to do, and you won't be out of place because many (though not all) of the other tea takers will be dressed up, too. Although opulent, the Brown Palace warmly welcomes children, and servers are adept at keeping them intrigued by reeling off interesting facts, including hints about the upside-down panels (see Hey, Kids!). However, good behavior and respect for the other diners and the elegant furnishings is expected, so if your brood is not yet ready to sit through the proceedings, save this treat until they are.

BUFFALO BILL MUSEUM & GRAVE

Buffalo Bill was a larger-than-life hero who epitomized the spirit of the Wild West, and the colorful stories kids will learn about him at this small museum are as likely to fascinate them as any of the actual items on display. Born in Iowa in 1846, William F. Cody left his childhood home in Kansas at the age of 11 to become an ox-team driver, going on to herd cattle, drive wagon trains, mine gold, ride for the Pony Express, and scout for the army. He gained fame as a skilled buffalo hunter, but he's probably best remembered as the consummate showman who brought the life and times of real cowboys and Indians to stages as far away as Europe. In spite of his reputation as a successful cavalry scout and a hunter who killed more than 4,000 buffalo in one eight-month period, Cody became an outspoken advocate for Indian rights and animal conservation. "Every Indian outbreak that I have ever known has resulted from broken promises and broken treaties by the government," Cody said. He also spoke out for women, saying in 1894 that the majority of them were "as well qualified to vote as the majority of men."

HEY, KIDS! Buffalo no longer roam wild in the West, but 30 of them (they're more accurately called American bison) live in pastures along I-70 today, 5 miles west of the museum near the Genesee Park exit. This herd, started by the city of Denver back in 1913, is directly descended from the last wild bison in the world. Look for the "Buffalo Herd Overlook" signs. The bison have their own tunnel under the highway, so they might be on either side of the road. The best seasons to spot them are spring, fall, and winter, when they're fed not far from the highway.

Older kids can learn all about Buffalo Bill through old photographs, posters, and extensive written material—there's lots to read here. Some of the artifacts, especially Sitting Bull's bow and arrow and Buffalo Bill's saddles and showy beaded costumes, are likely to interest all ages. The Native American exhibit is also very good, though primarily for school-age kids and older. Young children will probably be happiest hanging out in the Children's Corral, where they can dress in cowboy hats, boots, and bandanas, ride a fiberglass horse, and make their own "brands" with stamps. The setting alone is reason enough to come. Strolling up to the grave and around the grounds is a fine way to spend a sunny day, whether or not you linger in the museum.

EATS FOR KIDS

Historic **El Rancho** (29260 U.S. Hwy. 40, 303/526–0661), near the museum off I–70, serves lunch and dinner. Pizza, corndogs, grilled cheese, and chicken fingers ($4.50–$5.95) are available for kids, along with grilled quail, buffalo, burgers, fish, and prime rib for all. Save room for peanut butter pie or cinnamon bread pudding.

KEEP IN MIND

The museum has special events throughout the year, and these may be the best way to introduce Bill Cody to younger children. Native American families perform traditional music and dance at some events, and live buffalo, long-horn steer, or pack mules are often present for close encounters. There are always character actors on hand, so you can "meet" Buffalo Bill and Annie Oakley, among others, and chat with them awhile. Events celebrate Cody's birthday in February, the anniversary of his burial in June, and the holiday season on the first Sunday in December (free to Colorado residents).

BUILD-A-BEAR WORKSHOP

Although some mall-based hands-on chain establishments for kids are nothing more than marketing ploys, Build-A-Bear Workshop gives you a genuine feel-good experience—even if you have to pay for it. The good news is that you don't have to pay a lot (although you can); prices are such that kids can easily save up for bears on their own. And once a child has a bear, you have gift opportunities for years to come in the form of bear clothing and accessories. It's a surprisingly rewarding way to spend an hour or two with kids, a great venue for a birthday party, and a place where grandparents and grandchildren can have creative fun together.

Here's how it works: starting at the Choose Me station, the child and a "Master Bear Builder" (store clerk) select a bear (or another animal), then go through subsequent stations where the new friend is stuffed, stitched, fluffed, dressed, and named. You and the kids

EATS FOR KIDS For fun: **Rainforest Café** (in the mall, tel. 303/355–8500), where moderately priced pasta and chicken are secondary to waterfalls and bird shows. For fabulous food: **Roy's** (in the mall, tel. 303/333–9300), with upscale, kid-pleasing Pacific/Euro dishes, including a Bento box with teriyaki, salmon, and more to share.

HEY, KIDS! Check out the Build-A-Bear on-line site where you can contribute your own bear stories and artwork. The site includes an expanded version of the *Beary Newsworthy* newsletter, with articles, games, and jokes. Want to send an e-card? Just click on Fun & Games—there are cards for parents and grandparents, for birthdays, anniversaries, and any other occasion you can think of. And there are monthly contests you can enter to win a free bear. Note: *always* check with parents before giving your address or other personal information on the Internet.

help all along the way, choosing a heart and kissing it before it's placed in the bear, deciding how much stuffing you want, picking out clothing, choosing a name that's then entered into the store's computer, and so on.

It might sound gimmicky, but it isn't—really. Part of the credit goes to the people working in the store, who have a contagious sense of excitement about the project and, most important, show total respect for kids' choices and fantasies about their furry friends. And credit also goes to the concept itself: creating your own unique toy with its own story is something you can't do in many places no matter how much money you spend. The bottom line: you and the kids are likely to walk out of the store feeling good.

KEEP IN MIND The downside of taking kids to malls is dealing with the dreaded "gimmes." You can get around this situation by using the store as an opportunity to teach kids how to manage money and use their math skills. If you're paying, decide how much you're willing to spend, then give that amount—and no more—to the kids. They'll have to figure out how to stay within their budget. They'll also learn about making choices—a lesson that will serve them well long after they've left this particular store.

BUTTERFLY PAVILION & INSECT CENTER

The Butterfly Pavilion & Insect Center is relatively small compared to city zoos, science museums, and aquariums, making it perfect if you have limited time. It's also ideal for families with very young children, because you can see the exhibits while maintaining nap and meal schedules. All of which is not to say that this is a tiny place—and as of 2003 it will double in size, to about 33,000 square feet. (Check the Web site to see if the new building has opened.)

The pavilion has three major areas, devoted to butterflies, insects, and sea invertebrates. Though the touch tank is popular, the space for invertebrates of the sea isn't nearly as interesting or inviting as those for the insects and butterflies. (In the new building, the invertebrate section should benefit from the addition of jellyfish and octopus tanks, among other things.) In the "crawl-a-see-em," otherwise known as the insect center, there are enough creepy-crawlies to fascinate adults and kids, and easy-to-use magnifiers let you zoom in on the various inhabitants. Some of the insects are startlingly

HEY, KIDS! You can't go to the Butterfly Pavilion without stopping to meet Rosie, the Rosehair tarantula from Chile. Her furry little legs will tickle your hand, and she's as nice as she can be. Actually, there are several tarantulas the pavilion uses for hands-on meet-and-greets—and they're *all* named Rosie! The Rosies are between 2 and 25 years old and they've all shown a fondness for, or at least a lack of concern about, walking on humans. Most of the hand-held tarantulas are Rosehairs, but there are a couple of Mexican Fire-Knees, too. Which kind do you want to hold?

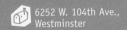 6252 W. 104th Ave.,
Westminster

 303/469-5441;
www.butterflies.org

 $6.95 ages 13 and up,
$3.95 ages 4–12

 Daily 9–5

 All ages

beautiful, others hideously ugly, and between signage and knowledgeable staffers, there's lots to learn.

Try to be in the tropical rain forest when keepers let the newest butterflies go. (You might have seen them emerge from their chrysalises in the viewing area dedicated to the miraculous process of metamorphosis.) The times for releases are posted; it's a good idea to claim your space a little early because this event can draw a crowd. Staff members talk about each type of butterfly before they release it, and often these newest residents flutter close to—or land on—visitors before venturing farther. When the new building opens, the conservatory with its 80-foot-tall glass pyramid will be home to about 2,000 butterflies, an increase of 800 from the original facility. Outside nature trails and a butterfly garden offer space to stretch and run while still providing a learning experience.

KID-FRIENDLY EATS There's currently a snack bar at the pavilion; a restaurant is slated for 2003. For an early dinner, though, try **Trail Dust Steak House** (tel. 303/427–1446; www.traildust.com) on U.S. 36 at Sheridan. Kids' entrées include ribs, chicken, steak, and shrimp ($4.99–$5.99), but the main attraction is the cool story-tall slide. Don't forget to bring along old neckties. Refuse to remove them and staffers will snip half off (the walls are covered with them), because at the Trail Dust, they don't cotton to formality! Kids find this tradition highly amusing, and you get a free drink for each tie.

CASA BONITA

59

Opinions vary about the quality of the food at this monstrous Mexican restaurant (52,000 square feet, seating for 1,100); some think it's little more than standard cafeteria fare, while plenty of others, especially younger diners, are considerably more enthusiastic. But it's not the food that makes Casa Bonita so popular. You should try it just for the experience—and once you have, chances are you'll find yourself going back, because kids get a real kick out of it. Out-of-town guests find it fun, too.

The cavernous space is designed to look like a Mexican village at night (regardless of what time you visit), with a plaza, a wishing well, caves, and vineyards—think Disney south of the border. Try to get a table with a good view of the faux-Acapulco cliffs, where a waterfall drops 30 feet into a small lagoon (you'll have to arrive early); every five minutes or so cliff divers do their thing, and staged scenes, such the "Black Bart" shoot-out—

KEEP IN MIND Black Bart's and the caves can be scary. There are glowing skulls, bats, and other frightening effects. Stay nearby at least the first time your children explore. Some kids also hide by the bridge specifically to scare others, so warn your children ahead of time.

EATS FOR KIDS The Little Amigos menu has a Mexican plate, cheeseburger, and chicken strips to choose from ($2.99). Older kids and parents will probably go for the ever-popular all-you-can-eat extravaganza of chicken or beef tacos and enchiladas, with rice, beans, guacamole, sour cream, and (yummy) sopaipillas for dessert (all for $8.99). Still hungry? Just raise the flag at your table and one of the 500 waitpersons (200–300 in winter) will bring you more for as long as you keep asking. There's a "gringo" menu for those who don't want Mexican.

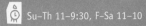 6715 West Colfax Ave., West Denver

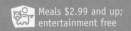 Meals $2.99 and up; entertainment free

 Su–Th 11–9:30, F–Sa 11–10

 303/232-5115;
www.casabonitadenver.com

All ages

culminating with the bad guy taking the plunge—are enacted every 15 minutes. (The fireflies by the cliffs are also a nice touch.)

There's so much action going on around you—strolling mariachi bands, puppet shows, magicians, an escaped gorilla (don't ask), flame jugglers, and more—that kids hardly have a chance to get restless. The flip side? This isn't the place for anyone who suffers from sensory overload. Children probably won't spend a lot of time at the table; they'll want to be checking out the mine and climbing through Black Bart's Hideout and the caverns (no, the bats and boiling mud pots aren't real). After eating, the whole family can dress up in Old West costumes and strike a dramatic pose for a souvenir "old-fashioned" instant photo portrait (for an extra charge).

HEY, KIDS! Here are a few fun facts about Casa Bonita, just in case you were wondering: the ice machine is 2½ stories tall, the bean kettle holds 200 pounds of dry beans, the dish-washing machine is 6 feet tall and about 20 feet long, and the tower is 85 feet tall, capped by a 22-karat gold leaf dome. The statue on top of the dome is Cuauhtemoc, the last Aztec emperor. Casa Bonita is the largest restaurant under one roof on the North American continent.

CELESTIAL SEASONINGS TEA CO.

What started with a young man and some friends picking wild herbs and hand-sewing them into bags has turned into America's largest herbal tea company, whose beautifully designed boxes are sold around the world. Celestial Seasonings says its aim is to "nurture people's bodies and uplift their souls." You get the feeling there's something to that when you tour the Boulder headquarters, what with the peaceful herb garden and scads of inspirational signs.

The tour begins with a tea tasting, followed by a brief film in the gallery, where original box art is on display. Once inside the factory, everyone has to wear hair (and possibly beard) nets, which amuses kids greatly. A favorite stop is the Mint Room, where crates of peppermint are stacked floor to ceiling. One whiff instantly clears your sinuses, if not, as the company believes, your mind. (Some people find this room too much, so be prepared for a quick exit.) The factory is the real thing, not a simulation, and you don't watch

HEY, KIDS! Go onto the company's Web site, click on Just for Fun, then click on Coloring Book. From there you can download some of the tea box artwork and color it yourself. The art selection changes periodically, but look for Sleepytime and Grandma Bear if you're 5–9, Chamomile and Bengal Spice if you're a little older or if you like the challenge of coloring more fanciful, complex drawings. Part of Celestial Seasonings' company mission is to create products that are "beautifully artistic." Maybe you'll design one of their tea boxes one day, and then millions people will see *your* artwork!

 4600 Sleepytime Dr., Boulder

 Free

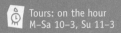 Tours: on the hour
M–Sa 10–3, Su 11–3

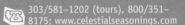 303/581–1202 (tours), 800/351–8175; www.celestialseasonings.com

 5 and up for factory portion of tours, all ages otherwise

from behind glass. You and the kids actually walk through the production area to see firsthand how tea is processed and packaged. Machines whir and music blasts as your perky guide tells you that approximately one million tea bags are made and boxed there each day. You'll also learn that by not putting strings with labels on most of its bags, the company saves two million pounds of paper per year.

The tour runs about 45 minutes, and guides encourage questions from everyone. It ends in the gift shop—no, there's no way around it, but high-quality products are for sale rather than tacky souvenirs, and teas are discounted. You can sample as many teas as you wish; kids seem to have no problem tasting their way through the entire line, even if you never knew them to be tea drinkers before.

KEEP IN MIND
The entire production crew takes a mandatory two-week vacation in July. The tours still run and you still walk through the production area, but you don't get to see the machines at work dumping tea, pressing it into bags, and boxing it to be shipped.

EATS FOR KIDS You need look no further than the **Celestial Café,** serving breakfast and lunch. Lunch items include sandwiches, burgers, soups, salads, and desserts ($2–$7). Some dishes are made with tea. In nice weather, sit out on the patio where views of the Rocky Mountains provide an impressive backdrop for your meal. The café is closed weekends, but sandwiches and cookies are available in the tour lobby. If you want to know how to make your own dishes with tea, log onto the company's Web site, click on Just For Fun, then choose Recipes to see which goodies are being showcased.

CENTRAL CITY OPERA

Central City is a small mining town 40 miles west of Denver with a big commitment to opera. Its opera company has been around since 1932, making it the fifth oldest in the country. Each season the company presents three operas, most often two classic productions and a third that's avant-garde or in some way groundbreaking.

The classic operas are usually chosen for the season's two youth performances, which feature talented apprentice singers rather than the regular cast but use identical staging and costumes. The big difference is that during youth performances a narrator comes out between acts to talk to children about the show and clarify what's going on in the story. There's nothing boring, pedantic, or patronizing about the way it's done, and kids won't feel like they're in school. On the contrary, the narrator gets the kids interested, makes them laugh, and ultimately gives them a familiar framework for understanding and appreciating the opera. As a result, children often come away with the surprising

KEEP IN MIND It's completely safe to wander the Central City cemeteries. The surrounding hills are not recommended for hiking, however, because of old mine shafts going hundreds of feet down. Even cars have fallen into shafts, so stick to roads and trails; tell kids to do the same.

HEY, KIDS! Check out the famous Teller House Hotel, next to the opera house. It's known for its Face on the Barroom Floor painting (painted in the 1930s and you can still see it today), and for many well-heeled guests. Back in 1873, President Ulysses S. Grant arrived for a visit, and miners laid a path of 26 solid silver ingots from the street to the hotel door for him. At the time, Congress was deciding whether gold or silver should back the dollar (gold won), and Grant refused to walk on the path so as not to show favoritism.

 124 Eureka St., Central City

303/292-6500, 800/852-8175;
www.centralcityopera.org

 $39–$69; youth perfor-
mances $10 adults, $5
students; parking $10
per car

June–Aug, evening performances 8,
matinees 2:30

6 and up

understanding that opera is for everyone—even them! After the show, the performers appear
in the courtyard to sign autographs, answer questions—and give kids an up-close look at just
how much makeup stage artists wear.

If the youth performance dates don't work for you, consider any of the matinees. There's
no narrator, but you can get a brief synopsis of the story on the opera company's Web site.
And the visit to Central City is interesting in and of itself. Many historic buildings—including
the opera house, which was originally constructed in 1878—still stand along the town's
narrow, twisting streets, giving it the feel of the19th-century mining town it once was.
Not long ago all of the opera house's old (read highly uncomfortable) seating was replaced
with 550 plush theater seats, which goes a long way toward making kids happier
operagoers.

EATS FOR KIDS Bring a picnic and eat in a historic cemetery
before the performance. There are a couple to choose from—just head west
up Eureka Street to the edge of town. People often died young in the 1800s
and early 1900s, and kids will find the historic markers and headstones interesting to read. (An annual event with character reenactments takes place in
the cemeteries each fall.) Restaurants in town come and go frequently, usually following the erratic fate of the area's gambling casinos.

CHAUTAUQUA ASSOCIATION & AUDITORIUM

Once there were Chautauquas across the United States; Theodore Roosevelt called them "the most American thing in America." Today, only three remain, and the Colorado Chautauqua is the only one west of the Mississippi. In operation since 1898, it continues the Chautauqua aim "to foster a variety of recreational, educational, social, cultural, and artistic programming for the community." It's a place to enjoy a spectacular outdoor setting and take in many of the area's best cultural events, from concerts and movies to classes in the arts. On Chautauqua's wide lawns you can picnic, read, meet with friends, and let the kids run around, and you'll find perhaps the best views of the mountains and sunrise and sunset in all of Boulder.

The main area, rising on a hillside above the city, includes gardens, trails, historic buildings, and a popular playground. Chautauqua Park, which spreads into the surrounding foothills, is part of the Boulder Mountain Park system, and has miles of hiking trails, from easy to challenging. Good trails for families are the 2-mile-long

EATS FOR KIDS The historic **Chautauqua Dining Hall** is open for breakfast, lunch, and dinner, with a children's menu for all three meals. Selections for breakfast—served until 2 PM—include *very* green eggs and ham and Mickey Mouse pancakes ($2.95–$3.95); the dinner menu has favorites such as mac & cheese, spaghetti, chicken fingers, grilled cheese, and burgers ($2.95–$4.95). Sadly, the famous Sunday brunch is now a buffet, but it's some consolation that now hungry kids can eat almost as soon as they sit down. (The nearby playground can also keep them occupied.) Dinner reservations are a good idea.

 900 Baseline Rd., Boulder

 303/442-3282;
www.chautauqua.com

 Park free, program
fees vary

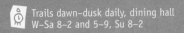 Trails dawn–dusk daily, dining hall
W–Sa 8–2 and 5–9, Su 8–2

All ages

Enchanted Mesa Loop (start at the Ranger Cottage), and the Chautauqua/
Bluebell/Baird Loop (head west through Chautauqua Meadow). Harder trails reward
hikers with views of awesome geological features, such as Royal Arch. Get maps
and information from the Ranger Cottage.

Chautauqua is probably best known for its concerts, and many family-friendly
programs are on the schedule. Each summer the Family Fest features music,
puppetry, and storytelling, and many of the regular concerts, from bluegrass to
jazz to classical, appeal to families. And there's more than just music. The annual
Silent Film Festival, also a family favorite, proves to today's high-tech kids
that movies don't need razzle-dazzle special effects to be fun. Parents of infants
to preschoolers should check out Chautauqua's experiential music classes, some
for parents and kids together, others just for kids.

HEY, KIDS! At the
Silent Film Festival, you see
movies the old-fashioned way:
without a soundtrack. Movies
were invented in France in the
1880s; in 1989 Thomas Edison im-
proved the technology with his
Kinetoscope. Movies were silent
until 1927, when *The Jazz Singer*
broke the sound barrier.

KEEP IN MIND Before heading to trails—even short ones—stop at the
Ranger Cottage to pick up trail maps and ask rangers about the various routes. Don't
rely on friends' suggestions; what's easy to one hiker is a challenge to another, and
when it comes to taking kids into the mountains, you want to be prepared.
Rangers know these trails and they've witnessed many, many families on them, so
they can give you the best advice. Be honest about your abilities, and they'll help
you decide on a trail that's appropriate and safe for your group.

CHATFIELD STATE PARK

Southwest of Denver, close to the mountains, is a park with one of the largest lakes in the metro area, covering 1,550 acres. Though just 15 miles from the city, Chatfield State Park has a wild feel to it, more so than its sister park to the east, Cherry Creek (*see #54*). In addition to the lake, one of the main attractions at Chatfield is birds, and lots of them. More than 340 species have been spotted here (though, sadly, the Great Blue Herons that populated the Heron Rookery have moved). But it's not just birds that are flying at Chatfield: model-airplane pilots have their own space, complete with a paved runway, just south of the campgrounds near the middle of the 3,768-acre park. If you want to see land-based wildlife, the best place is in the 28-acre preserved wetlands on the park's west side. Possibilities include beavers, muskrats, deer, coyotes, and foxes.

EATS FOR KIDS Picnic at any of the 139 picnic sites throughout the park, or just head to the swim beach and order from The **Candy Man** concession, where hot dogs, brats, and sandwiches top the menu ($2–$3.50). Soft drinks and sno-cones are available, too ($1–$1.50).

HEY, KIDS! Volunteer to be your family's safety expert. Remember that Colorado weather is unpredictable and high altitude can affect you if you're not used to it. Before hitting the trails, check that your group has: (1) a trail map and compass; (2) extra clothing and rain gear; (3) plenty of drinking water; (4) an emergency kit with flashlight, fire starter, matches in waterproof container, pocket knife, whistle, and a signaling device, such as a mirror; and (4) a small first-aid kit.

11500 N. Roxborough Park Rd., Littleton

303/791-7275;
www.coloradoparks.org

 $4 per car or $40
for an annual pass to
all Colorado state parks

 5 AM–10 PM daily

All ages

Chatfield has extensive facilities—boating, swimming, hiking, and horseback riding (livery, tel. 303/933–3636) are all available. No matter if you don't have your own boat. You can rent one (tel. 303/791–6104), or just sit and watch the busy comings and goings down at the marina, something young children never seem to tire of. The park's 18 miles of trails can accommodate hikers and cyclists, and mountain bikes are permitted. Whichever kind of bike you have, thorn-proof tires are recommended.

Consider taking a real break from the city with an overnight stay in the park; there are 163 campsites, some for tents only, some for families with recreational vehicles. The park also has ranger programs, but only for groups and schools. Come winter, Chatfield attracts outdoor-loving families with ice skating, ice fishing, and cross-country skiing.

KEEP IN MIND Other than at the swim beach, where no animals are permitted, dogs are welcome to join you at Chatfield. They must, however, be kept on a leash no longer than 6 feet. There is one place within the park where they can run—over in the dog training area located near the dam. Even though your pooch can be off the leash there, it still must be under voice control, and rangers do occasionally watch to make sure that that is the case.

CHERRY CREEK STATE PARK

Cherry Creek, about 13 miles from downtown in southeast Denver, is a haven within the boundaries of the city. It's 3,305 acres of prairie, wetlands, gently rolling hills, and cottonwood-shaded trails, with a panoramic view of the mountains, from Pikes Peak in the south to Longs Peak in the north. It feels at once close to and removed from the city.

The park is a year-round playground, with swimming, boating, hiking, and cycling in summer and ice skating, ice fishing, and cross-country skiing in winter. (With no snowmobiles allowed, the skiing is peaceful.) If bird-watching interests your kids, stop by the park office for a list of birds to watch for. Burrowing owls (look for signs of them near old prairie dog holes) are among the more than 150 migratory and resident species that have been sighted in the park; there are even raptors (bald eagles and peregrine falcons). You and the kids can also learn about the park's wildlife and ecosystem on ranger-

HEY, KIDS! Going out on ice? Remember: (1) always go with an adult; (2) bring along a rope, a cell phone, and a whistle in case of emergencies; (3) wear a life vest over your clothes; (4) walk at least 10 yards apart; (5) if a pet falls in, get help—don't try to rescue it; (7) if you fall in, stay calm and blow your whistle to get others' attention; (7) if you can pull yourself out, don't stand up—slide forward on your stomach to distribute your weight over a greater surface area.

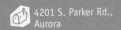
4201 S. Parker Rd.,
Aurora

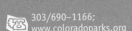
303/690–1166;
www.coloradoparks.org

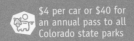
$4 per car or $40 for
an annual pass to all
Colorado state parks

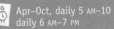
Apr–Oct, daily 5 AM–10 PM; Oct–Apr,
daily 6 AM–7 PM

All ages

led interpretive walks (call to arrange two weeks in advance). More than 100 deer call the park home, as do rabbits, coyotes, beavers, muskrats, raccoons, and weasels.

At the 880-acre reservoir, you can boat, water-ski, and take sailing lessons (call the marina, tel. 303/779–6144). Cherry Creek is one of the only state parks in Colorado with sailboard rentals; if your family wants to try the sport before investing in equipment, this is the place to do it. The park has 9 miles of bike trails (mountain bikes are allowed) and 12 miles of hiking trails; the trail system connects to the Denver Highline Canal Trail, with many miles of paths to explore. There are also trails for horses—contact the livery stable (tel. 303/690–8235) to arrange a ride. If all that's not enough for you, stop by the rifle range (tel. 303/693–1765) or the model airplane field.

KID-FRIENDLY EATS There are two food concession stands. One is located at the marina on the west side of the lake, the other at the swim beach on the northeast shore. Both offer typical snack bar type food, such as hamburgers and hot dogs ($2 and up).

KEEP IN MIND Because Cherry Creek State Park is so convenient to Denver, lots of people visit it—more than 1.5 million a year. The park is especially crowded on weekends and holidays, and in order to protect the environment and preserve natural resources there's a carrying capacity (a maximum number of visitors allowed), which is enforced. You're better off going to the park during the week, but if weekends or holidays are your only option, arrive early to avoid being turned away once the maximum has been reached.

CHILDREN'S MUSEUM OF DENVER

It's not surprising that a museum founded by parents and teachers places an emphasis on education; but listen to the giggles and laughs that emanate from the Children's Museum of Denver and you'll know this is a place where learning is fun. There are two major exhibits, intended for two different age groups. In the Center for the Young Child, children from infancy to age 4 take part in activities that enhance sensory awareness, large motor development, social and emotional growth, and cognitive learning. It has four exhibit areas: the Pond, for children up to 9 months old; the Meadow, for those 8 to 18 months; the Grove, for ages 16 months to 3 years; and the Village, for 2½ to 4 year-olds. In each area activity cards suggest how adults can guide children as they grasp, pour, and stack objects, climb in a "fort," dress-up, and role-play. Adults must accompany babies in play at the Pond and the Grove.

On the second floor of the museum, the Assembly Plant is a place where 4 to 8 year-olds can learn about teamwork and safety, among other things. It's truly hands-on,

KEEP IN MIND The museum has extensive resources and programs for parents and caregivers. An Early Childhood Workshop Series, Music and Movement, and other classes help adults gain a better understanding of the young children in their lives.

HEY, KIDS! You've probably learned about places that are "environmentally friendly." The Assembly Plant at the Children's Museum is one of those places. All of the tools and materials available for designing and building objects are 100 percent reused. They've been donated by people who don't need them anymore—so no new resources or materials are required. It takes one million of these "recycled" objects to keep the Assembly Plant fully stocked. You and your family can help by donating things you no longer need. Then other kids can use them, change them, build with them, and have fun with them.

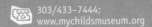 2121 Children's Museum Dr., Downtown

303/433-7444;
www.mychildsmuseum.org

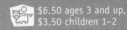 $6.50 ages 3 and up,
$3.50 children 1–2

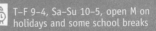 T–F 9–4, Sa–Su 10–5, open M on
holidays and some school breaks

 8 and under

with 12 workstations and bins of recycled household materials (donated by visitors, members, and staff) waiting to be made into any object a child can imagine. If kids are stumped for ideas, they can follow provided "blueprints."

The museum also has changing exhibits and special events that take place regularly throughout the year. The events are usually great fun: typical are Shaving Cream Creativity—a hit with toddlers—and the Sunday family program in which parents and their kids (ages five and older) use real tools to build small-scale houses, which they then played in. The museum gets very crowded, especially mornings, so staff recommends visiting between 2 and 5. That's nap time, of course, but if an afternoon works for your schedule, it's good advice.

EATS FOR KIDS You may not want to go farther than the **Hungry Tummy,** the museum's café (with a patio that has views of Denver and the mountains). The menu includes sandwiches, fruit, cookies, and other snacks (50¢–$6.00). If you decide to head into LoDo or central downtown, consider **Dixon's Downtown Grill** (1610 16th St., tel. 303/573–6100) for breakfast, lunch, or dinner. Adults can order fish flown in fresh daily, steaks, salads, and southwestern entrées, while the children's menu includes grilled cheese, eggs and bacon, and fish-and-chips ($3.50 with drink and ice cream).

CLEAR CREEK RAFTING

Rafting is, in every sense of the word, a cool way to spend a hot summer day. It's an activity for all kinds of families—those used to open-air adventure, but also those who don't have a lot of experience in the great outdoors. Truth to tell, on many rafting trips you don't need experience or skill, just a willingness to go with the flow while guides handle the maneuvering. And parents whose preteens and teens complain that family outings are "*sooooo* boring" will likely get a different response to the suggestion of river rafting.

There are several fabulous rivers only a short drive from Denver, among them Clear Creek, 25 miles west of the city. Of the companies organizing trips, Clear Creek Rafting is the most established, offering more excursions at more times throughout the day than anyone else. The river has awesome white water, with more challenging rapids per mile than just about any other commercially rafted river in the state. That doesn't mean it's

EATS FOR KIDS Head to Idaho Springs on I–70 just west of rafting headquarters. **Buffalo Restaurant & Bar** (1617 Miner St., tel. 303/567–2729) is famous for breakfasts and buffalo-meat dishes of all kinds. There's a typical kids' menu ($4.50), but try something buffalo. **Beau Jo's** (1517 Miner St., tel. 303/567–4376) serves "mountain pizza pies" (thick rolled crust filled with your choice of seven unusual sauces and 30-plus toppings). No slices here, but there's a kids' menu and a salad bar for kids (about $1.29–$3.49). Colorado honey on the table lets you turn leftover crust into a scrumptious dessert.

out of bounds for beginners and younger children. Easy sections of the creek are tame enough for families with kids as young as 7, yet still provide some mini-thrills over roller-coaster rapids. Other stretches are not for the faint of heart. With names like Double Knife, Hell's Corner, and Terminator, these monster rapids require good conditioning and some experience—in other words, they're perfect for thrill-seeking teens who have spent some time on the water. If the parents want to join in, so much the better.

Beginner trips start in the daytime or early evening, last several hours, and include 11 fun rapids. Half-day intermediate and full-day advanced trips have a minimum age of 15—although depending on conditions, minimum ages can change, so check ahead. Whichever trip you choose, the scenery will be stunning and the kids will be impressed with their adventurous parents.

KEEP IN MIND
Wetsuits, life vests, and helmets are provided. Bring: athletic shoes and wool socks; fleece, polypropylene, or wool outer-wear (no cotton); and towels and dry clothes for after the trip. Good sunglasses that block UV rays are imperative for kids and adults; bring a high SPF sunscreen.

HEY, KIDS! There are 11—count 'em, 11—rapids on the beginner section of Clear Creek ranging from Class I to Class III. What does that mean? Most U.S. rafting outfitters use a six-class system to describe rapids, with Class I being frothy, fast-moving water and Class VI being unrunnable (a raft can't safely negotiate it). Intermediates on Clear Creek whoosh through Class III and IV rapids, while advanced trips challenge experienced water rats with big waves and drops rated Class IV and V.

COLLAGE CHILDREN'S MUSEUM

Collage is a small museum with an unassuming location in a corner of a Boulder shopping plaza that belies the quality of its offerings. The size makes it perfect for young families—it's well contained and not too overwhelming—and younger children will get the most out of it. However, the museum also serves kids in its older range as a place to spend an hour or two when the urge to be creative hits.

Making believe is big here. Visitors can become actors in impromptu theater productions, pretend to be emergency workers and police officers (including police artists who construct computerized images of missing persons), or play the role of cook, waiter, or customer at an imaginary diner. Creativity is emphasized, but one of the things Collage does extremely well is mix pretend activities with valuable information about the real world. While pretending to be emergency workers, for example, kids learn how to call

KEEP IN MIND Collage has Free Friday Fun Nights on the first Friday of every month. Hours are 5–8, and families can join in all of the regular museum activities. Collage also runs special programs with other local cultural groups, such as the Shakespeare Festival (see #47).

HEY, KIDS! Collage displays artwork of local school children in its Art Gallery. If you go to school in Boulder, your work might be on display some day. If you're just visiting the area, check out the gallery. Are you doing the same kinds of things in your school? Does Collage's Art Gallery give you any ideas for your own artwork? Many great artists have found inspiration in the works of other artists, and art students spend many hours in museums studying famous paintings and sculptures. Maybe something in Collage will inspire you!

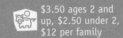 2065 30th St., Boulder

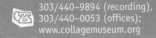 303/440-9894 (recording),
303/440-0053 (offices);
www.collagemuseum.org

 $3.50 ages 2 and
up, $2.50 under 2,
$12 per family

M and W-Sa 10-5, Su 1-5

 9 mths-9 yrs

911, a potentially life-saving skill. A traveling aquarium sponsored by the City of Boulder Water Quality Services teaches children about the connection between clean water and healthy fish. And there are a variety of science-related exhibits and special programs, such as Sensational Science Saturdays. (Yes, finding out why balls roll at different speeds in Roller Race is really a lesson in physics.)

The practical lesson may not be so significant at the Frozen Shadows exhibit, where you "capture" your shadow by moving between a light source and a phosphorescent screen, but it's something that both kids and adults seem to love. Maybe that's because it makes everyone who takes part feel and act like, well, a kid. In the final analysis, Collage might not rival some of the bigger, splashier children's museums in the country, but it does a fine job on a small scale, and it's popular with many young families.

EATS FOR KIDS **Golden Lotus** (1964 28th St., tel. 303/442–6868) is a good Chinese restaurant just a couple of blocks from Collage. Avoid Boulder's ever-increasing lunchtime traffic by taking a shortcut: go through the back of the museum parking lot, around Target, through the south end of Target's lot, and park in the lot adjacent to the restaurant. It's two minutes, no lights, no wait. Lemon chicken is highly recommended by kids in the know, but just about anything you order here is fine (lunch entrées $6.25–$7.95), and food generally comes quickly—a plus for hungry kids on the verge of cranky.

COLORADO GOVERNOR'S MANSION

If you want to see a grand historic house still in use, rather than turned into a museum piece, this is your chance: 400 E. 8th Avenue is home to the governor of Colorado and his family, and should someone in your family become governor one day, it's where he or she will take up residence. The house's primary appeal to kids may simply be the fact that the governor actually lives here. Beyond that, it's unlikely to engage younger children or those without any interest in architecture or period furnishings. Families with kids who have either studied Colorado history or learned a little bit about art and architecture, however, may enjoy checking out the public rooms and collection of artwork from around the world. Tours start every 10 minutes and only last about half an hour, so this isn't a big time commitment.

The Colonial Revival mansion was built in 1908 by Walter Cheesman, one of Denver's early settlers and its first pharmacist. He died before it was completed, but his wife and daughter lived here for several years before selling it to Claude Boettcher, another well-

EATS FOR KIDS   **Govnr's Park** (672 Logan St., tel. 303/831–8605) is named for its proximity to the mansion, just across the street. While evenings bring a young adult crowd for the tavern and poolroom, this is a great place for families, too, particularly at lunchtime. The kids' menu includes quesadillas, grilled cheese, and burgers (about $3.50); adults have burgers and other typical tavern fare to choose from. The poolroom is generally empty during the day, and the tables are free until 4 PM, making this a good alternative to more kid-oriented restaurants with arcade games. In summer, the shaded front patio is nice.

known name among the early elite of Denver. The Boettcher family donated the mansion to the state in 1960. It became a historic landmark in 1969 and underwent an extensive renovation in 1999. Today you can tour the elegant Palm Room, which opens to one of the nicest features of the mansion, the terraced garden designed by Cheesman. There's a large library, an ornate dining room, and the requisite grand staircase leading up to the family quarters.

What will probably capture the imaginations of kids, who often have a penchant for things ornate and elaborate, are the extravagant furnishings and art pieces, most notably an 1800 Waterford crystal chandelier that once hung in the White House and an Italian marble nymph and porpoise statue. There's also a collection of exquisite jade and quartz sculpture, another chandelier (18th-century French), a huge tapestry, a hand-carved Italian Baroque marble-top credenza, and a Louis XIV desk.

HEY, KIDS!

According to the Colorado Historical Society, Colorado's first serious crime occurred in 1859, when John Stuffle shot his brother-in-law, Arthur Binegraff, and stole his gold dust. Justice was swift and harsh. Stuffle was arrested the next day and hung the day after that.

KEEP IN MIND These tours are hosted by volunteers of the Colorado Historical Society, folks who are passionate (and fairly serious) about Colorado history. They want to share all they know about the house, its artwork, and the people behind it all, so good listening skills are definitely a requirement. There's nothing hands-on or interactive about the tour, so if your kids would rather be someplace where they can touch things and behave like kids (and who can blame them), wait on this tour until they're older.

COLORADO HISTORY MUSEUM

Miners, pioneers, fur trappers, Indians, soldiers, industrialists, outlaws—these were early residents of Colorado. The state's history is full of colorful characters and innovative thinkers who left their mark on the land and culture. The Colorado History Museum preserves their stories—of love, loss, discovery, invention, and progress that came with a price.

The collections are composed of artifacts, photos, and documents, and though there are some large, eye-catching pieces—such as a full-size covered wagon and massive mining equipment—much of what's best about this museum is in the written material accompanying exhibits. Signage is extensive, meaning families with older children will get the most out of the experience. The 150-year timeline of Denver is primarily text and photographs, and kids who take the time to read it all will be rewarded with lots of fascinating facts, as well as legends and lore. There isn't much hands-on here, but the mining area, where

EATS FOR KIDS Café **Odyssey** (500 16th St., tel. 303/260–6100), on the other side of the Civic Center from the museum, features three dining rooms with fun themes. An extensive menu has pizza, sandwiches, steaks, and pasta; the children's menu includes chicken, burgers, spaghetti, and grilled cheese ($2.95).

HEY, KIDS! In the late 1800s divorce was a scandal. No scandal was bigger than the one caused by Horace A. W. Tabor, who made his fortune mining silver in Leadville and became one of Denver's most prominent early citizens. A multimillionaire, he divorced his wife, Augusta, and married a young divorcee known as "Baby Doe." Augusta lived through the scandal but never recovered from it, and Baby Doe froze to death next to the mine that Horace left her on his deathbed. Two of the three died penniless, one died a millionaire. Find out who's who at the Colorado History Museum.

 1300 Broadway, Downtown

 $4.50 ages 13 and up, $3.50 ages 6–12

M–Sa 10–4:30, Su 12–4:30

303/866-3682;
www.coloradohistory.org

8 and up

you can walk up and down ramps looking into the gigantic machinery, is a big draw for kids at the younger end of the age range.

Although you might never know it from traditional schoolbooks, much Western history includes not only whites and Native Americans, but blacks and Hispanics as well. To its credit, the Colorado History Museum devotes lots of space to every group. Of all the things to see at the museum, the most moving might be the video of descendents of the Sand Creek Massacre of 1864 retelling the stories of relatives who were there. It's not easy to watch or listen to; what happened at Sand Creek, mostly to Cheyenne women and children, is horrific, so be prepared to talk to your children about it. Nevertheless, the video and the Cheyenne Dog Soldiers exhibit of which it's a part are excellent. In addition to permanent exhibits, the museum also hosts a variety of temporary shows—some more engaging for kids than others.

KEEP IN MIND In summer additional family programs are added, including a day camp for kids. In 2001, for example, Hit the Road, for ages 8–12, met for five days; each day the group traveled to local historic sites and had pre- and post-travel fun at the museum. History Express has been another successful summer program—it's one of the few hands-on areas for kids (making it great for younger visitors), with costumes to try on, games, crafts, and more. Each week the historical themes change, and the costumes and activities along with it. The staff hopes to make History Express permanent.

COLORADO RAILROAD MUSEUM

There's a natural connection between kids and trains—engine to caboose, full-scale train or miniature model version, they all seem to capture the imaginations of boys and girls, to say nothing of adults. And that makes the Colorado Railroad Museum a great destination for families. Set on 15 acres about 12 miles west of downtown Denver and 2 miles east of Golden, the museum has more than 70 historic narrow and standard gauge locomotives and cars on exhibit, as well as thousands of rare old photographs, artifacts, and documents that bring to life Colorado's railroad history.

Railroads were crucial to Colorado during the late 1800s when gold and silver were discovered in the mountains. Isolated mining towns rose overnight, and railroads were their lifelines. More than one boomtown turned ghost town when railroads were diverted or stopped running. Most of the old lines are now obsolete, but there's a lingering romance associated with them that appeals to young and old. The museum building is a replica of an 1880-

HEY, KIDS! Go on a train hunt. Find the oldest authentic Colorado locomotive; it's on display at the Colorado Railroad Museum. Here are some clues: it was built in 1880. It was originally numbered 51 when it ran on the Denver South Park & Pacific line. It went on to be numbered 191, 31, and 7 on different lines in two different states. When it was 52 years old, it was finally retired and put on display at a logging museum. Can you find it?

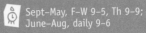
style depot, and though you should spend time wandering around inspecting the photos and documents, kids will want first and foremost to be outside looking at the trains themselves. They're full of character: once you read their fascinating histories, they take on their own unique personalities. A visitor's gallery allows you to watch ongoing restoration projects.

Don't miss the Denver HO Model Railroad Club's facility on the lower level of the museum, or the Denver Garden Railway Society (DGRS) G-Scale Exhibit behind the museum. The latter is an outdoor exhibit of models running through a miniature landscape; some engines even puff steam (although they're actually electrically powered). DGRS members are often there running the trains—and always on "Steam Up" dates, when the museum runs its working steam engines on the tracks around the grounds.

EATS FOR KIDS

There's a shaded picnic area at the museum; bring coolers and food—but no alcohol. **Jake's Diner** (17695 S. Golden Rd., tel. 303/278–9805), open for breakfast and lunch, is a short drive and nothing fancy—just decent food at great prices ($3 and up).

KEEP IN MIND You can rent the big red caboose for birthday parties or special events. It's available year-round and holds about 25 people comfortably. The cost for parties is $100 and includes admission to the museum for all of your guests. The museum will clean up the caboose and get it ready for you, then put a sign on it for the day saying that it's closed for a private event. They don't supply anything other than the caboose, though; you have to bring your own supplies, including food, plates, and utensils.

COLORADO SHAKESPEARE FESTIVAL

The Colorado Shakespeare Festival (CSF), heralded by the *New York Times* as one of the top three Shakespeare festivals in the nation, opened in 1958, making it America's second oldest. Each season four plays are put on—three in the Mary Rippon Outdoor Theatre, one in the University Theatre. Comedies are definitely the better choice for younger kids, and there's at least one every season. Try for a show with lots of slapstick and physical comedy; kids love it, and they can understand what's going on even if they don't follow every twist of the plot. You can help engage kids by taking advantage of CSF's preshow programs, including Elizabethan entertainment on the "green" and backstage tours ($5, free with highest-price tickets) where kids learn about the creation of that night's performance and see firsthand how the actors prepare. Sometimes a visit to the costume and crafts area is included.

The outdoor venue is far better for kids, particularly younger ones. Whispers and squirming are a little less noticeable, and there's an added sense of adventure and fun when

HEY, KIDS!

Shakespeare is famous for making up lots of words. He's credited with introducing some 2,000 words into the English language, including *submerged, gloomy, leapfrog, lonely, puke, snail-paced, alligator, anchovy,* and *eyeball*. His longest word? *Honorificabilitudinitatibus*, from *Love's Labour Lost*, meaning really, really honorable.

KEEP IN MIND

The language of Shakespeare can be a challenge, and the plays, particularly comedies, often have mind-bogglingly complex plots. Before going, look together at the synopses on CSF's Web site. And check bookstores and libraries for kids' guides, including *Bravo, Mr. William Shakespeare!*, by Marcia Williams (Candlewick Press); *All the World's a Stage*, by Michael Bender (Chronicle Books); *The Young Person's Guide to Shakespeare* (with CD-ROM), by Anita Ganeri (Harcourt Brace); *Shakespeare for Kids: 21 Activities*, by Colleen Aagesen and Margie Blumberg (Chicago Review Press); and *Shakespeare Stories*, by Leon Garfield (Houghton Mifflin).

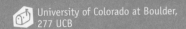

you see Shakespeare under the stars. Comfortable kids are happier kids, so bring cushions or stadium seats for the stone benches, or rent stadium seats there. All seating is assigned, so there's no need to come early to compete for a prime spot. Of course, weather is a factor, early evening thunderstorms being common in Colorado. Bring rain jackets or umbrellas and wait it out; the show will most likely go on. And make sure kids are well rested—shows don't end until late in the evening.

CSF also has summer day camps for kids. A three-week session for ages 11–16 includes workshops on costume, set design, playwriting, and the ever-popular stage combat, and a weeklong camp for kids 8–10 is held in conjunction with Collage Children's Museum.

EATS FOR KIDS Bring a picnic and join other theatergoers on the green (the lawn between the two theaters), where performers entertain from 7 to 8 (6:30 to 7:30 in August) with Elizabethan music and song; Will Shakespeare himself may even appear. If you don't want to pack a picnic, order **Falstaff's Fare** ($12 each) with your tickets or at least 48 hours before the performance. Dinner consists of salmon, chicken, or vegetarian entrée with baguette, butter, and fruit. You can buy drinks and desserts in the **Bard's Yard** courtyard where you pick up your meals. Food isn't allowed in the theaters.

COLORADO STATE CAPITOL

46

Colorado's State Capitol building took 22 years to construct and is modeled after the U.S. Capitol in Washington, D.C. There's a big difference, though: Colorado's Capitol dome is covered in gold. Real gold. It's much thinner than tissue paper and was applied in rolls. When the dome was regilded in 1991, it took 160 rolls to cover the 2,842 square feet—but only 47 ounces of gold total!

That's just one of the cool facts you'll learn touring the Capitol. You can explore the building on your own, but you'll have richer experience on the guided tours, which provide lots of interesting details. Even better, the kids can ask questions of the guides, who know an amazing number of facts. Some of this won't be interesting to younger kids, but still the tour is well worth taking. From an architectural standpoint, the Capitol is exquisite. It's filled with Colorado marble (even though shipping marble from Italy apparently would have been cheaper than digging it out of the local mountains) and so much native rose

HEY, KIDS! Denver is the Mile High City, and for years the 13th step on the west side of the Capitol was thought to mark the exact mile-high point. Lots of tourists took pictures of it. Then some curious engineering students from Colorado State University decided to check the accuracy of the marker—and guess what? It wasn't a mile high, proving that grown-ups are sometimes wrong, too. (The students benefited from better measuring equipment than had been used before.) A "geodetic survey plug" is now embedded in a different step to indicate the real mile-high point. Can you find it?

200 E. Colfax Ave., Downtown

 Free

 June–Aug, M–F 9–3:30, Sa 9:30–2:30; Nov–Dec, M, Th, F 9:30–2:30, T, W 9–2:30; Jan–May, M–F 9–2:30; tours every 30 min

303/866-2604

8 and up

onyx that the state's entire supply was depleted. Kids are usually impressed to learn that the granite walls are 5 feet thick and that the cornerstone, at the northeast corner, weighed a hefty 20 tons in its rough state. Check out the eight murals on the first floor, which tell the story of Colorado in picture and verse; see if your kids pick up on the fact that almost every panel stresses the importance of water to the West.

It's most fun to visit the Capitol when Congress is in session (mid-January–mid-May) so you can watch the political process in action. Show your kids the state flag and ask them to guess what the colors stand for: blue is for Colorado skies, gold for the precious metal, white for mountain snow, and red for Colorado soil.

EATS FOR KIDS
Check out **Wolfe's Barbecue** (333 E. Colfax, 303/831–1500), about a block from the Capitol. No kids' menu, but they'll suit portions to any size child. Ribs are tops, but the barbecued tofu is right up there. Prices range from $3 to $8.

KEEP IN MIND Don't miss touring the dome if you're in reasonably good shape, but be aware that the climb is a challenge, up a total of 93 steps starting from the third floor on the north side of the building. If you've just arrived in Colorado and aren't yet used to the high altitude, save exploring the Capitol until you're acclimated. Otherwise, you'll be trying to catch your breath at the top of the dome rather than enjoying the stunning city and mountain views from 272 feet up. For the best views, wait for a clear day.

COOKING SCHOOL OF THE ROCKIES

At the Cooking School of the Rockies there are classes for every level of cook, from the culinary-impaired to the aspiring professional chef—and for every age level, too, including kids. The classes are taught by working chefs and caterers, and are divided into three categories: demonstration, tasting, and hands-on. Naturally, classes for kids and families are hands-on all the way.

The course offerings vary throughout the year, but typical of those for kids is Camp Kitchen, for ages 8–12. This three-hour class covers kitchen safety, rudimentary culinary skills, and preparation of simple, kid-pleasing foods. Among the creations that have been taught are sky-high sandwiches, munchable crunchables with ranch dressing, pile-it-on dip, homemade nacho chips, oven-fried chicken, and cookies. Teen classes, for ages 12–15, can be either basic or more advanced. Examples of the former category are Teens in the Kitchen, which demonstrates techniques for slicing, chopping, baking, roasting, and

HEY, KIDS!

Eggstremely Interesting Fact: in Denver, due to the high altitude, water boils at 202 °F instead of 212. So what? That means it takes 4 minutes to cook a soft-boiled "3-minute" egg and 17 minutes for a hard-boiled egg—5 minutes longer than at sea level!

EATS FOR KIDS
In hands-on classes, the end of the class is devoted to sitting down as a group and eating the fruits of your labor. The worktables are set and stools are pulled up so you can enjoy your creations together and talk about what you like and what you might improve on next time. If, for some reason, you think your child would love taking the class but might not like the food (unlikely, as the school has a good idea of which foods kids enjoy), pack a snack.

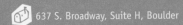
637 S. Broadway, Suite H, Boulder

Classes from $40 to over $500; most family classes $40–$80

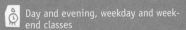
Day and evening, weekday and weekend classes

303/494-7988;
www.cookingschoolrockies.com

8 and up (younger for some parent-child classes)

sautéing, and Pasta for Teens, which teaches how to create such colorful dishes as silk handkerchiefs with pesto, bowties primavera, and meat and cheese ravioli. In Teen Tech, a four-hour class on three consecutive Saturdays, kids find out how to prepare more complicated dishes, from sautéed pork chops with caramelized onions and cider to spinach salad with warm bacon vinaigrette to chocolate mousse. Along the way they also learn about shopping and organizing a kitchen and pantry (skills a parent can love). Sometimes a holiday is the focus, such as the Mother's Day for Kids class, in which 8- to 12-year-olds learn to whip up a delectable breakfast for Mom.

In addition to courses aimed strictly at kids, the school occasionally offers classes the whole family can take together. There's cooking, to be sure, but this family time is also about communicating and bonding in a fun and positive way.

KEEP IN MIND Older kids with a strong interest in cooking and experience in the kitchen can also take some of the regular courses with an adult. Talk to instructors before signing up to make sure the course is appropriate. A grown-up and older teen might also consider one of the multiday "vacation courses." For most classes, students are expected to bring their own aprons. For teen and adult classes, students are usually asked to bring along a favorite knife as well. If you don't have one, check out the school's excellent store, the Chef's Market, on the premises.

COORS FIELD

Ever wanted to walk through a real major league baseball dugout or clubhouse? Or wondered what the field looked like from the press box? Or maybe just speculated about whether the view from the luxury suites could possibly be worth the price? Here's the chance for you and the young baseball fans in your life to find out all that and more, at one of the most fun ballparks in America.

Coors Field, which opened in 1985, is a modern stadium designed to feel like a traditional ballpark. While it captures that old-timey charm, it incorporates facilities that fans of yesteryear would never have dreamed of, including many intended specifically for families. On the hour-and-15-minute tour, given year-round, you'll go behind the scenes and learn about the stadium's construction and its numerous special features. You'll see a lot of it firsthand, including the visitors' dugout and clubhouse (if there's no game that night)

HEY, KIDS! There are a couple of cool things to notice about Coors Field. First, there's a row of purple seats that stand out. They're at exactly 5,280 feet above sea level—in other words, one mile high. Second, if you know anything about Colorado you know that it can snow at just about any time. The designers of Coors Field knew that, too, so they put a heating system *under the field.* As soon as a flake hits the ground, it's gone. Now that's cool.

 2001 Blake St., LoDo

 Tours and general information
303/ROCKIES or 800/388–ROCK;
www.rockies.mlb.com

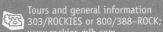 Tours $6 ages 13 and up,
$4 ages 12 and under;
games starting at $4 ages
13 and up, $1 ages 12
and under

 Tours Apr–Sept, M–Sa 10–3, 10–1 before night games, no tours before day games. Oct–Mar, M–Sa 11–2

 Tours 5 and up,
games all ages

and the suites. The tour is good for all ages; the guides welcome kids wholeheartedly and will change the focus of their talks a bit when children are in the group.

If you go to a game, be sure to take a walk around. You can circle the entire stadium on the concourse without missing a play, and there are lots of kid-friendly amenities, including batting cages and other games on the outfield concourse and a playground behind left field (section 148) where small children can run and climb. You'll also get a great view of the bullpens. Of more practical interest, every men's, women's, and family rest room has diaper-changing facilities. Bottom line: Coors Field is a great place for families and kids. Going to a game is a fun outing even if you're not the biggest fan—and for those who *are* big fans, the tour can be a thrill.

EATS FOR KIDS
There's good food—really—at Coors Field. But if you want to go beyond that, consider **Breckenridge Brewery** (2220 Blake St., tel. 303/297-3644) a short hop away. It serves casual fare—chicken, salads, soups. The kids' menu includes corn dogs, chicken strips, and fish-and-chips ($3.25).

KEEP IN MIND You can walk in and sign up for a tour that day, but you might not be able to go exactly when you want to. On busy summer days, tours can sell out—each one accommodates a maximum of 38 people. It's a good idea to book your tour in advance by calling the number above and requesting a specific day and time; you can pay by credit card. Arrive at the stadium a little early to pick up your tour tickets.

CULTURAL CONNECTION TROLLEY

43

Denver's Cultural Connection Trolley (CCT) is not an attraction in itself, at least not exactly. And it's not really a trolley—it's a bus. But it's a kid-friendly, kid-pleasing way to get to many of Denver's great family attractions: there are no long walks to and from parking lots, kids don't have to be confined, and all views are good views. Children who don't spend much time on buses also like the novelty. For parents, riding CCT means not having to figure out how to get from one place to another in a city with many oddly angled and confusing streets.

CCT stops at almost every city attraction that's of interest to kids. Your all-day pass allows you to get on and off either of the two routes as many times as you like—so, for instance, on the Green Route you can hop from Larimer Square (*see #22*) to the State Capitol (*#46*) to the Museum of Miniatures, Dolls and Toys (*#39*), before taking in Molly Brown's house (*#19*). Take the Red Route to drop in at the Denver Art Museum (*#42*) and the Public

EATS FOR KIDS Many of the Denver restaurants mentioned in this book are on or near the trolley routes, including Wolfe's Barbecue near the Capitol, Palette at the Art Museum, Racine's near the Mint, Maggiano's Little Italy near the 16th St. Mall, and Pasta, Pasta, Pasta near the Tattered Cover in Cherry Creek.

HEY, KIDS! What's with those Denver streets, anyway? Most of the city is laid out in the traditional way, with streets running north–south and east–west. But in the heart of downtown, the original part of the city, the streets run at an angle, southeast to northwest and southwest to northeast. It's said that early surveyors, after studying the climate, came to the conclusion that having streets at such an angle would allow a portion of every building to be bathed in sunlight for part of each day. Of course they didn't know that one day Denver would have huge skyscrapers, making the issue irrelevant.

Trolleys start at intersection of 14th and California Sts., Downtown

 $3

 May–Sept, daily 9:30–6

303/299–6000 RTD; 303/892–1505 or 303/892–1112 Convention & Visitors Bureau

All ages

Library (*#36*) before heading over to Cherry Creek for shopping and a bite to eat. The trolleys on the Green Route start at 14th and California streets, with the first leaving at 9:30 in the morning and the last at 5:30 in the afternoon. They complete a course of approximately 16 stops in about an hour. The Red Route also starts at 14th and California, beginning at 10. Trolleys take an hour to complete the route of about 12 stops, and the last one leaves at 6 PM.

Buy passes directly from the driver (exact change is required); from Regional Transportation District (RTD) stations at the Civic Center, Market Street, DIA, Longmont Terminal, or Boulder Transit Center; or from Denver Convention and Visitors Bureau outlets at the Tabor Center and Cherry Creek Shopping Center. Ask for a map and schedule, too.

KEEP IN MIND Your all-day Cultural Connection Trolley passes are also accepted on Denver's other transportation systems, including the light rail and RTD local buses. You can connect with a variety of routes throughout the metro area and use your pass to get back to your home or hotel after you've finished sightseeing. For information on Denver's RTD options, go to www.rtd-denver.com. You'll find all the information you need on bus and light rail routes, but as of this writing, there was nothing on the site about CCT.

DENVER ART MUSEUM

F ew art museums are as thoroughly child- and family-friendly as this one, which is known particularly, but not only, for its superb collections of Native American and Pre-Columbian art. No matter which of the seven floors you find yourself on, there are places and special elements designed to intrigue and educate kids.

On the 7th floor, devoted mostly to Western art, there's a Discovery Library in which kids can dress up as *vaqueros* (Spanish cowboys), unlock an old safe to discover period artifacts, and rummage through the desk of an Old West painter. While kids learn and play, parents can relax on big leather couches. In the 6th floor Discovery Library, there are more dress-up opportunities and a castle to explore via CD-ROM. There are also Art Stops (open generally on weekends)—hands-on stations with objects to touch and helpful people to answer questions. All of the museum's collections are appropriate for families—the Native American gallery is a favorite—and even special exhibits include elements for kids. Typical

HEY, KIDS! Log onto www.wackykids.org, the museum's site for kids. You'll find cool stuff to look at and activities to try, like making masks and origami (projects change with the museum's exhibits, but they're all fun). Just download the instructions and begin creating. Most you can do yourself, but there are some projects you'll probably want a grown-up to help with—the museum tells you which ones. Sometimes there's even stuff like free museum passes (good for the whole family) to download, and you can always find out about books and other Web sites you'll probably like.

was the 2001 Winslow Homer show, at which sketch pads and pencils were placed throughout rooms so kids (and adults for that matter) could try their hand at replicating the artist's work.

You can't see everything in a day, so choose one or two floors to concentrate on. Before starting, pick up a discovery backpack for kids in the lobby (available weekends and daily in summer at no charge). Each pack has objects and activities related to particular exhibits. (It's hard to resist the Asian pack with its sushi box lunch set.) Leave time for the Just For Fun Center on the lower level (weekends and daily in summer), where families can create their own postcards, build giant puzzles, and more; this is a great spot for very young children.

EATS FOR KIDS

Palette, at the museum, features creative cuisine by Kevin Taylor, one of Denver's top chefs. If you want to introduce kids to fine dining in the daytime, make reservations. Casual **Palette's Express** has sandwiches and salads; the kids' meal deal ($3) includes sandwich, fruit, and drink.

KEEP IN MIND The museum schedules weekend family workshops throughout the year, generally for either 3- to 5-year-olds or 6- to 8-year-olds accompanied by an adult. Recent workshops have involved such activities as making prints, and creating Japanese "treasure bowls," and turning ordinary objects into art. Sleepovers for ages 8–12 are usually on the calendar, as are multi-day camps during school breaks. All workshops and camps include exploration of the museum itself, so kids can find inspiration for their own masterpieces. And Saturdays are always free for Colorado residents.

DENVER BOTANIC GARDENS

41

In its literature the Denver Botanic Gardens describes itself as "a collision of art and science," and that perfectly defines what the place is all about. Spread over 23 acres adjacent to City Park, it's both a beautiful urban oasis and a living laboratory for learning and discovery—a combination that makes it not only one of the top botanic gardens in the country, but also a place where both parents and kids want to be.

There's an emphasis on plants specific to Colorado and the Rocky Mountains, but flora from all over the world is represented. In total, some 15,000 species can be found, both indoors and out. In winter the Tropical Botanica, with banana trees and other exotic life forms, is a balmy haven from cold weather. In warmer months the outdoor paths and gardens range from regional landscapes such as the Plains Garden and Sacred Earth (inspired by the heritage of Native Americans from the Four Corners area) to the more lush Spanish

EATS FOR KIDS A mile from the gardens is **Gunther Toody's** '50s retro diner (4500 E. Alameda, tel. 303/399–1959). It's a fun place with classic American fare at nearly retro prices ($5–$10), including fabulous old-fashioned milkshakes. On the kids' menu: burgers, hot dogs, and pasta ($3).

HEY, KIDS! Japan is famous for its serene, peaceful gardens. Using plants, rocks, and often water, Japanese designers try to show the harmonious relationship between humans and nature. Go to the Japanese Garden at the Botanic Gardens. Look around, then close your eyes. Listen. Smell. Did the garden engage all of your senses? Does it make you feel peaceful and in harmony with your surroundings? This garden is called Shofu-en, meaning Garden of Pine Wind. In Japan, the pine tree signifies long life and happiness. Why do you think they chose the pine tree to represent those things? What tree or other plant would you choose?

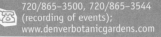 1005 York St., City Park

 720/865-3500, 720/865-3544 (recording of events); www.denverbotanicgardens.com

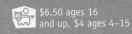 $6.50 ages 16 and up, $4 ages 4–15

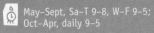 May–Sept, Sa–T 9–8, W–F 9–5; Oct–Apr, daily 9–5

All ages

Orchard and the pool of the Monet Garden crowded with water lilies; the Japanese Garden is award-winning. If you dream of having your own garden but lack the space, become a member and rent one of the 200 10- by 15-foot plots in the Community Gardens ($55, sign up in spring).

Kids will waste no time discovering the hidden paths, tunnels, and mazes of the Children's Secret Path, and they'll be happy to know that there are plans for a full-fledged Children's Garden and a Family Learning Center. Call to find out about concerts in the gardens; some are held on free days (3rd Monday of the month, April–October). Finally, while gift shops are often more a detraction than attraction, this one is excellent, with unique, high-quality products for all ages, so set aside a little time and money and stop by before leaving.

KEEP IN MIND There are many special programs for families, mostly in spring and summer. A summer KidCamp has weekly sessions for three age groups: 7–8, 9–10, and 11–12. Kids can also take one-day workshops on such topics as Bugs and Butterflies, Science in the Garden, Your Secret Garden (starting your own), and Express Yourself (journaling and painting). There's storytelling on weekends throughout summer, as well as special events like the Mad Hatters Tea Party. Teens and Moms might enjoy the workshop for adults on making your own face and skin care products. Fees range from free to $219.

DENVER FIREFIGHTERS MUSEUM

This is one of Denver's real museum gems. Its home, Fire Station No. 1, was built in 1909, and at the time it was one of the largest firehouses ever in the region—two stories and 11,000 square feet, including three stables and a hay loft for the horses who pulled the engines. Hard though it is to believe today, Fire Station No. 1 once served all of downtown Denver. Over the years, as horses were replaced by motors, it was modernized, until in 1979 it was finally decommissioned and soon thereafter opened to the public.

Today, the station serves not only as a museum dedicated to preserving and presenting the history of fire fighting in Denver, but also as a repository of historic information for the Denver Fire Department. It contains lots of antique equipment and historical displays—the station itself is a museum piece, listed on the National Register of Historic Places, with the original poles and much of the original woodwork intact—but it's also happily

EATS FOR KIDS **The Hard Rock Cafe** (500 16th St., tel. 303/623–3191), on 16th and Glenarm, is always a favorite, and it's a short walk. You know the menu—burgers, etc. There's a standard kids' menu, too ($6.99). If you're in the mood for Italian, try **Maggiano's Little Italy** (500 16th St., tel. 303/260–7707), also in the 16th Street Mall. It has checkered tablecloths, dark wood, and old pictures, plus good food in good-size portions. No kids' menu, but a family of four or more can order a family-style meal with kids 12 and under paying half price. Some half-portions are available, too.

 1326 Tremont Pl., Downtown

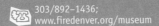 303/892-1436;
www.firedenver.org/museum

 $3 ages 17 and up, $2
ages 16 and under

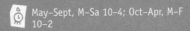 May–Sept, M–Sa 10–4; Oct–Apr, M–F
10–2

 All ages

hands-on, making it great for families with young children. The big stuff is what everyone likes best. The museum collection includes three hand-drawn "trucks" from 1867, a horse-drawn steam pumper from 1873, and three motorized trucks from the first half of the 20th century.

Little kids like putting on the real helmets and boots, to say nothing of climbing on an old truck and clanging the bell. Kids of all ages love sliding down the fire pole—not a real floor-to-ceiling one but a smaller, safer version. And older kids and adults studying the historical photos and literature will appreciate the difficulties early firefighters faced putting out deadly blazes with hand- and horse-drawn equipment and far less sophisticated pumping systems than we have today.

HEY, KIDS! In 1863 much of Denver was destroyed by fire. A year later, a flash flood in Cherry Creek caused death and damage. During the Civil War, a Denver volunteer army had to fight Confederates bent on taking the gold fields. Life was tough in early Denver!

KEEP IN MIND You can get to the Firefighter's Museum on the free 16th Street Mall Shuttle (*see #9*). Get off at Tremont Place and walk three blocks west to reach the museum. In summer months you can also get there via the Cultural Connection Trolley (*see #43*). Get off at 14th and California, walk three blocks east, and turn right on Tremont. Once at the museum, you're only one block from the United States Mint (on West Colfax, *see #5*), so it's easy to combine these two attractions in a day of exploring downtown.

DENVER MUSEUM OF MINIATURES, DOLLS & TOYS

It's hard to miss the Museum of Miniatures, Dolls & Toys: just look for the yellow cottage with the green roof and white fence on the east side of Gaylord Street. Once inside, you'll find permanent and changing exhibits of miniatures, dolls, dollhouses, toys, and teddy bears on display throughout, though the majority are up on the second floor. There are dolls from the 1700s to the present, made from just about any material you can think of, and originating from all around the world. One was given to Colorado by the Japanese city of Yokohama, which explains why the museum sometimes has workshops on Japanese dolls (*see* Keep in Mind). What many kids like looking at most, though, are the meticulously furnished and decorated dollhouses, from simple homes to multiroom mansions. Not surprisingly, some of the houses are representative of architectural styles specific to the American West, such as an adobe Santa Fe dollhouse and a miniature tepee set up in a detailed display with teeny, tiny Native American weavings.

EATS FOR KIDS Hop on the Cultural Connection Trolley (*see* #43) as it continues its loop, get off at E. Colfax and Detroit, and walk back three blocks. **Goodfriends** (3100 E. Colfax, 303/399–1751) has all-around good food and a kids' menu with ziti, burritos, grilled cheese, and more ($2.95).

HEY, KIDS! What makes the museum a cottage instead of a house? It's not about size, it's about location—when it was built in 1899 it was out in the country. At that time the city of Denver ended at Broadway and Colfax. Talk about change! Look over at City Park: today it's green with gardens, but in the 1880s it was mostly buffalo grass, sagebrush, and cactus. Now check out something cool inside the house, in the entry hall. Look at the brass outlet near the living room doors. What do you think that was for? (The answer is in the museum handout.)

 1880 Gaylord, City Park

 $5 ages 17 and up,
$4 ages 2–16

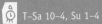 T–Sa 10–4, Su 1–4

 303/322–1053

 3 and up

The historic yellow cottage that's home to the museum is interesting in its own right; it's an excellent example of Dutch-Colonial Revival architecture with much of the original décor preserved. Take time to read the handout you receive when you enter and share it with your kids. It gives a brief history of the cottage, which was built in 1899, and then goes into detail about the rooms on the main floor, from the library to the butler's pantry and back staircase.

While the museum itself is very family-friendly, some of its visitors are not families but adults, such as collectors, with an interest in dolls and toys. They take dolls seriously and sometimes seem less tolerant of exuberant kids than you would expect in such a place.

KEEP IN MIND If you get together a minimum of 10 kids, you can make a reservation for a workshop. The museum runs a variety of them for ages 3–6, 7–10, and 11–14. Themes in the past have included animal and dragon masks, Japanese paper friendship dolls, finger puppets, antique-style model cars, cornhusk dolls, and detailed miniature landscapes. They cost $3 per child plus museum admission, and some fulfill requirements for Brownie, Girl Scout, and Cub Scout badges. Also ask about free-event days scheduled during the year, with hands-on activities and projects.

DENVER MUSEUM OF NATURE AND SCIENCE

Denver has the good fortune to be home to one of the largest, and one of the best, natural history museums in the country, where families have been learning about the natural world since 1908. The list of Kids' Top Five Favorite Things at the museum is headed by the Hall of Life, an interactive exhibition on human health and science—how the body works, how babies grow, what part genetics plays in looks and health, and how lifestyle choices affect well-being. Kids love learning how their favorite foods stack up nutritionally (often not well) and testing their physical abilities in the fitness section. Examining the effects of smoking, drugs, and alcohol on the body is very popular, especially the drunk-driving simulator (expect lines). Other exhibits in the Top Five are Prehistoric Journey, IMAX (which costs an additional fee), Egyptian Mummies, and, in a tie, Gems and Minerals and Animal Dioramas.

With all its glitter, the Gems and Minerals display catches the attention of even very young children. Among the highlights: the cherry-red Alma King, the largest and finest

HEY, KIDS! Want a challenge? Go on an elf hunt. One of the artists who painted the museum's diorama backgrounds hid small elves in his works. There are six visible throughout the museum—but they're really well camouflaged and almost impossible to find! Go ahead and try. For a little help (you'll need it), ask for the "Museum Seek-and-Find" sheet at the information desk. When you find one of the elves, don't tell anyone else—let your friends and siblings take the challenge, too!

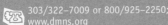 2001 Colorado Blvd., City Park

 $7 ages 13 and up,
$4.50 ages 3–12

Daily 9–5 (June–Aug, T 9–7)

303/322-7009 or 800/925-2250;
www.dmns.org

All ages

known rhodochrosite crystal on Earth. It was discovered in 1992 in a mine near Alma, Colorado. What's really fun is that, by sheer luck, a museum video crew was with the miners when it was unearthed, and you can watch the historic event on monitors.

That's just a small sampling of the wonderful exhibits here. Throughout the museum, look for Discovery Centers and Touch Carts where kids can try hands-on science and hold real museum objects. And a great museum is going to become even better: in 2003 a multimillion-dollar space science exhibition is scheduled to open, complete with a state-of-the-art planetarium and an astronaut training center where kids can try on a space suit and possibly even experience a low-gravity environment. In the world of museums, this is a don't-miss experience.

EATS FOR KIDS
The **T-Rex Café** has hot entrées, grilled sandwiches, pizza, a salad bar, a potato bar, and a burger/fries/toy kids meal ($3.50). The **T-Rex Deli** features made-to-order sandwiches, salads, pastries, and desserts ($4.50 and up). Go before 11:30 or after 1:00 to avoid the longest lines.

KEEP IN MIND
The museum has an extensive list of children's and family programs, from single-day parent–child workshops for ages 3–4 to multiday rafting, canoeing, and camping adventures in Colorado and beyond. If you can't get away for that long, check out the list of two- to three-hour field trips for families to nearby parks and other areas (primarily in summer). Children's camps and programs are available for kids in preschool through eighth grade. You can find out all of the current offerings on the museum's Web site.

DENVER PERFORMING ARTS COMPLEX

The Denver Performing Arts Complex is a four-city block, 12-acre site consisting of nine performance venues with combined seating of more than 10,000—more seats than any other similar complex in the U.S. except New York's venerable Lincoln Center. It's home to Denver's most prominent performing arts companies, including the Denver Center Theatre Company, Colorado Ballet, Colorado Symphony, and Opera Colorado. In addition, it has several educational components for aspiring and professional actors.

Like Denver itself, the complex is a melding of turn-of-the-20th-century historic buildings and state-of-the-art glass and steel facilities, and whether it's concerts, ballet, Broadway shows, or just about any other kind of live arts performance, you'll find it here. The annual list of shows is extensive, and there are always some productions geared to families. *Cinderella, Beauty and the Beast, The Lion King,* and *A Christmas Carol* have all been staged at the Complex in recent seasons. There are also shows not specifically aimed

EATS FOR KIDS **Rock Bottom Brewery** (1001 16th St., tel. 303/ 534–7616) is a brewpub, but it's great for kids. They receive crayons with their menu—which ranges from PB&J to pizza ($1.95–$3.95)— and things are lively enough that no one minds if kids make a little noise.

HEY, KIDS! Did you know that the Tony Award—like the Oscars but for plays instead of movies—is named after a Denver native? Unlike the Oscar, the Tony is named for a real person, Antoinette Perry. She was born in Denver in 1888, and from the time she was six wanted to act. Back then, acting wasn't considered proper for young women. Nevertheless, Perry became an accomplished actress and director and was much loved on Broadway. After her death from a heart attack in 1946, friends decided that an award named for her would be a fitting memorial.

 1245 Champa St., Downtown

303/893-4000;
www.denvercenter.org

 Ticket prices vary;
some free

Day, evening, and weekend performances

4 and up for some shows,
higher for others

at families but certainly appropriate for preteens and teens—*Cyrano de Bergerac* and *Riverdance,* for example. In 2001 a show called *Leader of the Pack,* featuring the rock/pop hits of Ellie Greenwich ("Be My Baby," "Chapel of Love," and "Da Doo Ron Ron," in case you've forgotten), was a kick for multiple generations to experience together.

If you're concerned that a family trip to the theater will break the bank—and there's no question that it *is* expensive—consider the "Free For ALL" matinees to selected shows from the Denver Center Theatre Company season (usually on the first Saturday of each show's run). Information about these shows is posted on the Center's Web site about a week before each performance, and local papers list the dates as well. Make no mistake, these are high-quality performances. The resident Denver Center Theatre Company, the center's professional resident company, received a Tony Award for Outstanding Regional Theatre in 1998.

KEEP IN MIND Parking can be a challenge in Denver. On performance nights, the Complex garage is often filled before seven o'clock. Try to arrive early, park, then go for dinner. If that's not possible, consider parking by Larimer Square *(see #22)* at the Market Street garage and taking the pre- and post-performance shuttle from Champion Brewery. In summer, you can also take the Cultural Connection Trolley *(see #43)* to the Complex, but you'll have to catch a cab back in the evenings. The Complex parking hot line, tel. 303/640-7275, will alert you to problems.

DENVER PUBLIC LIBRARY

The Denver Public Library (DPL) system collection includes more than five million items, and its Central Library is the largest public library between Chicago and Los Angeles. The city is justifiably proud of its library system—in a 2000 independent rating of public libraries nationwide, it was ranked #1 of all libraries serving populations over 500,000. The stunning 1995 addition to the Central Library is fittingly right across a small plaza from another of the city's architecturally distinctive buildings, the Denver Art Museum. Visiting both is a fine way for families to spend a day, and you won't hear any objections from the kids.

Architecture aside, the Central Library has a stellar children's collection. Children's books, videos, CDs, educational computer software, and reference services are all on the main level in one convenient area, and within the adult library there's also a designated Teen Space. In addition to the extensive collection of books and materials, there are plenty of other reasons to head to the library, including after-school programs, Read-Aloud visits

HEY, KIDS! To find out what's going on at the library, log onto the Web site. Kids' programs and other interesting things are listed. You can also click on Kids and find links to the DPL's favorite sites for animals, sports, science, Hollywood, games, and homework. There's even a list of best sites for toddlers, so if you have a little brother or sister, check out that list and write down the links for your mom or dad. Or better yet, go onto the sites and explore them with your sibling.

10 W. 14th Ave. Pkwy., Downtown

 Free

 M–W 10–9, Th–S 10–5:30, Su 1–5

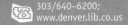 303/640–6200;
www.denver.lib.co.us

 All ages

from popular authors, Internet workshops, and Fabulous Family Weekend activities (listings are on the Web site). Typical of the events for kids are Jungle Joe's Critter Show, with live animals that you can see up close; storytelling; crafts; and performing artists such as jugglers and dancers. Recent events for teens have included Japanese Taiko drumming and a science/safety program about the brain and how a helmet can protect it (which included watching scientists dissect a sheep's brain!).

During school holidays there's usually something going on at the library. The computer terminals are another great resource, particularly if you don't have a computer at home or if you're traveling and your child wants to connect to the Internet. And you're always free to find your child's favorite books among the library's extensive collection, then curl up in a cozy corner and read together.

EATS FOR KIDS **Wazee Lounge & Supper Club** (1600 15th St., tel. 303/ 623–9518) may have Denver's best pizza ($4.95 and up); go weekdays—weekends are crowded and smoky. **Paramount Café** (511 16th St., tel. 303/893–2000) serves burgers and gumbo in a casual setting; there's a typical kids' menu ($2.75–$4.75).

KEEP IN MIND In order to borrow books from the Denver Public Library, you have to have a valid Denver library card, available at the circulation desk and free to Colorado residents. DPL also honors library cards from most other libraries across the state, so if you're from Colorado and will be visiting Denver, remember to bring your family's cards—you never know when you might need a good book. Out-of-staters can't borrow books, but will find plenty of worthwhile things to do on the premises.

DENVER ZOO

35

Spread out over 80 acres in City Park, the Denver Zoo has nearly 4,000 animals representing more than 700 species. It's the most popular cultural attraction in Colorado and has the seventh most diverse zoo population in the country—a far cry from when it opened back in 1896 with one orphaned black bear cub. Cubs have been a notable part of the zoo's history: in 1995 it garnered international attention when keepers hand-raised two polar bear cubs after their mother abandoned them. Against all odds, Klondike and Snow not only survived but thrived.

The zoo has major modernization and expansion underway throughout this decade. Although work is in progress, there's lots to enjoy. For interactive zoo-going, head to Bird World and help keepers feed the residents (usually at 2 PM, but ask). On the menu: mealworms and waxworms. Then take a spin on the fabulous Conservation Carousel, where

EATS FOR KIDS Your best bet for food at the zoo is the **Hungry Elephant** (near entrance, with the largest menu) or **Northern Shores** (by the seals and polar bears). The kids' meal at either is a hot dog or corn dog with chips and animal cookies ($4.50).

HEY, KIDS! When Mshindi (Swahili for warrior) was born at the zoo in 1993, who could imagine his extraordinary talents? Today, he's the world's only known artistic rhinoceros—you can see his paintings in the Pachyderm Building. Mshindi learned to paint as part of a behavioral enrichment program. He can also fetch a stick and sit on command. These skills aren't all fun and games; they help foster a positive relationship with his keepers, making it easier for them monitor his health, among other things. Other rhinos participate in the program, but none have displayed Mshindi's awesome talent.

 E. 23rd Ave. between York and Colorado, City Park

 Apr–Sept: $9 ages 13 and up, $5 ages 4–12; Oct–Mar: $7 ages 13 and up, $4 ages 4–12

 Daily; Apr–Sept, 9–6; Oct–Mar, 10–5

 303/376–4800; www.denverzoo.org

 All ages

instead of the traditional ponies and such you ride on depictions of 48 endangered and rare animals (one of the most popular is the mama polar bear with her two cubs); it's over in Pachyderm Park. To see a live endangered animal, visit the Western Lowland Gorilla exhibit and check out 25-year-old Koundu; he's 5-foot-2 and 535 pounds, making him one of the largest of his kind in captivity. Koundu's home is part of Primate Panorama, a 7-acre habitat closely replicating the natural environment of social primates; it's an innovative exhibit that's indicative of what's in store as modernization progresses.

Check daily schedules for Wildlife Encounters, where you can touch a skink (and learn what one is for that matter), cozy up to a chinchilla, and more. And the Denver Zoo was the first in the country to convert its diesel train to ecofriendly natural gas, meaning when your feet get tired you can take a ride and be kind to the environment.

KEEP IN MIND For the animals' safety and continuing good health, it's important to teach children never to throw anything into animal habitats—that includes coins in ponds and pools—and to discard all trash from picnics, snacks, and purchases so objects can't blow into exhibit areas. To counteract this perennial zoo problem, keepers have actually taught some animals to remove debris themselves. Sammy and Gidget, two of the zoo's sea lions, along with the orangutans, have learned to trade in found trash for treats. That doesn't mean, of course, that families should be any less careful!

DINOSAUR RIDGE

Waves once lapped the shores of an inland sea where tiny invertebrates burrowed into tidal flats and dinosaurs wandered the outlying swamps in search of food. Mangroves and other moisture-loving plants grew in profusion in a landscape that, unimaginably, would one day become dry and spectacularly mountainous. One hundred million years later, "one day" is now, and the place is Colorado.

Such sweeping geological changes are hard to grasp, but fortunately we have a visual record of them, less than 15 miles west of downtown Denver on a rocky ridge near Interstate 70. At Dinosaur Ridge, you can follow in the footsteps—literally—of creatures long gone from the Earth. You can see ripple marks left by waves and trace fossils of those tiny invertebrates. Finds at the ridge include Jurassic dinosaur bones and Cretaceous footprints, as well as a variety of plant fossils.

HEY, KIDS! After visiting Dinosaur Ridge do you have some questions about geology? No problem. First, check out the Dinosaur Ridge Web site and its links. If you're still stumped, try asking a U.S. Geological Survey scientist: send your question in an e-mail to Ask-a-Geologist@usgs.gov. Replies can take a few days, and they're only able to respond to about 45 percent of the questions they receive. (If you don't get an answer the first time, try again.) But don't expect them to answer test questions or write reports—they think you should do your own schoolwork.

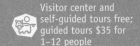

 16831 W. Alameda Pkwy., Morrison

Visitor center and self-guided tours free; guided tours $35 for 1–12 people

 Visitor center and gift shop 9–4 daily; often later in summer

303/697–DINO; www.dinoridge.org

5 and up

Begin at the visitor center, where exhibits set the stage for what's outside. Even young kids may find Dinosaur Ridge interesting, but school-age children will benefit most in terms of real learning. You have two choices for exploring. You can pick up a field guide at the visitor center and take a self-guided tour, stopping at the 17 interpretive signs that describe fossil remains and other geological and paleontological points of interest along the one-mile Dinosaur Ridge Trail. Or you can call a week in advance and enlist one of the volunteer guides, who will help you get a close look at the tracks and other highlights during a 1½-hour tour. Guides have lots of information about the area not necessarily included in printed field guides. Families can combine dino studies with a high-country hike by trekking up the 2-mile Dakota Ridge Trail that runs along the ridge crest, beginning near interpretive stop #8. Views are awesome, but bring water and wear sturdy shoes.

EATS FOR KIDS
Take a short drive to the **Morrison Inn** (301 Bear Creek Ave., tel. 303/697–6650) for moderately priced Mexican food. The kids' menu has quesadillas, burritos, and nachos as well as hot dogs and hamburgers ($2–$3). The potato chips are homemade and the margaritas are locally famous.

KEEP IN MIND During warmer months, generally May to October, Dinosaur Ridge has Discovery Days one Saturday each month. On those days guides stand at various points of interest along the route. You can go on foot or hop one of the buses that leave every 15 minutes from the visitor center parking lot ($2 per person). In summer the facility also has Dinosaur Ridge Science Day Camps for ages 8–10 and 11–13. Each session meets for a week and costs about $150.

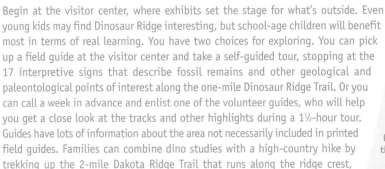

E-TOWN

Where can you take your kids to see the taping of a live radio show, with world-class musicians and the kind of variety and social commentary that made radio great way back when? Try Boulder, almost every Sunday night. E-Town generally tapes at the Art Deco Boulder Theater off the Pearl Street Mall, and it's proof that radio today isn't just about money, charts, and play lists.

There's an old-fashioned, homey feel to E-Town, due mostly to the husband-and-wife team of Nick and Helen Forster, the creative force behind the show. Making everyone—hosts, musicians, interviewees, audience, radio listeners, even advertisers—feel part of a close community is what the show is all about. Musical luminaries who have headlined include Mary Chapin Carpenter, Los Lobos, James Taylor, Lyle Lovett, and Sarah McLachlan. There are two music acts per show; in between, Nick Forster interviews writers, activists,

EATS FOR KIDS BJ's Pizza **Grill & Brewery** (1125 Pearl, tel. 303/402–9294) on the Pearl Street Mall is a friendly brewpub serving pizza, burgers, chicken, and excellent salads. The kids' menu has pizza, burgers, ravioli, and a sundae ($3.95). Sit on the patio for good people-watching.

HEY, KIDS! Do you know a local hero? Someone who has made a real difference in your town or community? You can nominate him or her for the E-Chievement award by going to the E-Town Web site. The nominee doesn't have to be an adult—kids have won the award, too. A 15-year-old Baltimore girl won because she'd been volunteering in soup kitchens since age 8, and at age 10 started her own organization to help the homeless. Before you make a nomination, be sure to read *all* of the rules.

politicians, and policymakers, from Jimmy Carter to Jane Goodall to Dave Barry. Kids see firsthand how radio shows are created, and when they clap with the rest of the audience (sometimes with a little encouragement from stage), they become part of the show. Each week E-Town also presents an "E-Chievement" award, recognizing people around the country "who have found positive solutions to problems and challenges in their communities." In other words, kids also see firsthand how a person or a group can make a difference.

E-Town isn't specifically for families, but there are always families in attendance. They get high-quality entertainment, positive messages, and a little education, with no violence, sex, or poor role models. It's something you and your kids can enjoy together—an all-too-rare commodity in entertainment today. Best of all, you can sit down again when the show airs (check the Web site for stations and times) and relive the experience.

KEEP IN MIND To find a radio station in your area that carries E-Town, go to the Web site and click on Radio Station. E-Town is broadcast on more than 100 stations in 34 states, the District of Columbia, and Guam; both commercial and National Public Radio stations carry the show. If it doesn't air in your town, contact E-Town and they'll tell you how to help make it happen. To see the show live, purchase tickets on the Web site or call the Boulder Theater (tel. 303/786–7030).

FAMILY SPORTS CENTER

amily Sports Center is both an entertainment complex and the practice facility of the Colorado Avalanche, the Stanley Cup–winning professional hockey team. In total, the facility at the intersection of Arapahoe and Peoria covers 140,000 square feet, including two ice hockey rinks and 37,000 square feet dedicated to family sports and entertainment, both indoors and out.

Sports and game enthusiasts of all ages can try out the heated driving range, 9-hole executive golf course, miniature golf, rows of state-of-the-art video games (it's almost overwhelming), a laser tag arena, and a climbing wall. For toddlers and preschoolers, there are little rides and a small gym. Ice rinks are usually open to the public twice each day. Naturally, there's a ton of golf and hockey merchandise to be had, and if you get hungry, you can choose between a snack bar and a full-service restaurant.

HEY, KIDS! Denver is one of only 10 cities in the country to have teams in all four major sports leagues: the NHL Colorado Avalanche, NFL Broncos, MLB Colorado Rockies, and NBA Nuggets. The Avalanche and the Nuggets play at the Pepsi Center, the Rockies play at Coors Field, and the Broncos recently got a new stadium, Invesco Field at Mile High (most people liked the old name Mile High Stadium much better). Can you name the other cities with teams in all four leagues? Denver also has a Major League Soccer team, the Colorado Rapids.

6901 S. Peoria St., Englewood

 Games $3 and up, multiple attractions $9.95–$11.95, Avalanche practices free

M–F 10–9, Sa 10 AM–11 PM, Su 10–8

 303/768-8303

2 and older

The Avalanche facility is on the west side of the complex. It houses the team's administrative offices as well as a dressing room and exercise and training areas available only to the team. One of the big draws here for hockey fans, especially younger ones, is the chance of seeing the Avalanche practice. The team doesn't post its practice schedule, so there's no guarantee of seeing them, but you can call ahead to the center and ask if they're there or if they're expected. The team's game schedule is posted on its Web site (www.coloradoavalanche.com); you can get a good idea of when they might be practicing based on when they're playing at home. In 2001, for the first time in four years, the team also held its preseason training camp at the Family Sports Center (rather than at a Colorado Springs facility). The camp schedule was posted in July, and it took place in September. This can be a great opportunity to get an up-close look at the team in action.

EATS FOR KIDS

For families on the go, the **Snack Bar** has typical fare—hot dogs, nachos, and pretzels ($1.50–$2.50). For a sit-down meal, consider the center's **Avalanche Grill,** serving a variety of all-American choices. Its children's menu features spaghetti, burgers, ravioli, and chicken fingers ($3.50).

KEEP IN MIND If your kids are big league sports fans, consider touring of Coors Field (see #44) or getting tickets to a Rockies game or a Nuggets basketball game—whichever is in season. The NFL Broncos also offer tours of their stadium (much easier to arrange than game tickets). You may have your best chance of seeing the Broncos in action at their training camp up in Greeley, north of Denver. You can check the schedules of all four of Denver's professional sports teams on their individual Web sites.

FISKE PLANETARIUM

On the campus of the University of Colorado (CU) at Boulder, Fiske is the largest planetarium between Chicago and Los Angeles. Star Shows in the planetarium theater are multimedia presentations on various aspects of the universe: Mars, the discovery of new planets, the Milky Way, and the massive collisions that have been going on in space since the dawn of the solar system. The shows last about 45 minutes and topics change, so call or visit the Web site for a current schedule.

Fiske's location at CU is a real bonus because audiences get to hear the insights of talented university professors and researchers who often "star" at evening Star Talks. The speakers make these talks interesting and enlighting to children. Topics range from locally oriented themes such as Boulder Skies—concerning what's coming up that can be viewed from the city and how best to make out the international space station—to more esoteric topics such as Organic Molecules in Space. In between are presentations such as one interpreting the skies from a Native American viewpoint.

EATS FOR KIDS

Mustard's Last Stand (1719 Broadway, tel. 303/444–5841) isn't just about hot dogs. There are excellent sandwiches, from charbroiled tuna and veggies (this is Boulder, after all), to sausage, chicken, and beef. Kids' deal: choice of dogs (even veggie) or burger with fries and soda ($3.09).

HEY, KIDS!

Don't miss the Colorado Scale Model Solar System, an outdoor exhibit on the CU campus. The sun and the four inner planets are near the planetarium entrance; the outer planets extend along a straight walkway. By odd coincidence, a street running through campus coincides with the location of the asteroid belt between Mars and Jupiter. The model demonstrates the inconceivably vast distances of our universe: each centimeter in the model represents 10 billion centimeters in the real solar system! The model is dedicated to CU alumnus Ellison S. Onizuka and the rest of the crew of the space shuttle *Challenger*.

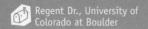 Regent Dr., University of Colorado at Boulder

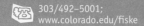 303/492-5001; www.colorado.edu/fiske

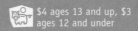 $4 ages 13 and up, $3 ages 12 and under

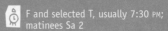 F and selected T, usually 7:30 PM; matinees Sa 2

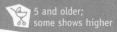 5 and older; some shows higher

One of the best things about Fiske—and probably the biggest draw for kids in the younger age range—is that after most evening presentations the audience can visit (at no extra charge) the adjacent Sommers-Bausch Observatory to look through high-powered telescopes trained on different parts of the sky. Helpers assist kids with focusing and adjusting. On Saturdays (and some weekdays in summer) the planetarium has science shows geared toward kids and families, and at Christmas there's a show that looks at the astronomical aspects of the holiday, including the star over Bethlehem. Before or after shows, wander around Fiske's lobby to check out the exhibits on meteorites, space toys, telescopes, sci-fi art, and more. And pick up an information sheet in the lobby with a map of the outdoor model solar system and tons of fascinating facts (see Hey, Kids!).

KEEP IN MIND The shows and talks vary in their appropriateness for different age groups, some being good for kids as young as 5, others better for middle-schoolers. Call ahead and ask the staff for an opinion—they've been presenting shows to families since 1976 and have a good idea of what works for which age group. In addition to show information and schedules, parents can also learn on the Fiske Web site about the many science programs and camps offered through CU. There are workshops for kids from 4-year-olds to teens.

FORNEY TRANSPORTATION MUSEUM

Dedicated to preserving and interpreting transportation history, Forney has what all kids love—things with wheels. They're housed in an airy 146,000-square-foot renovated warehouse, where there's still room to add to the collection that already includes hundreds of vehicles representing just about every mode of transportation known to humankind, from bicycles and buggies to automobiles and farm machines, from wagons to trains and planes. Among the favorites is the world's largest steam locomotive, the aptly named *Union Pacific Big Boy*, measuring 132 feet long and weighing in at a whopping 1,189,500 pounds. There are plenty of other trains, too, including railcars, cabooses, coaches, and a diner. In addition to the trains themselves, the museum provides details on both the history of the various cars and the railroads' impact on the development not only of Colorado, but of the entire West.

In the museum's extensive automobile collection are some names familiar to the younger generation—Ford, Chevy, Lincoln, Cadillac—and some from out of the past, like Studebaker

HEY, KIDS! The Packard Motor Car Company made some of the very first cars in the U.S., and it was the automaker that pioneered some of the things we take for granted today in our cars. According to the Packard Club Web site, a Packard was the first car to go faster than a mile a minute (60 miles per hour)—back in 1903! Packard put in the first backup lights in 1927, the first automotive air-conditioning in 1939, and the first automatic windows in 1940. For more information about this historic automaker, visit the Packard Club site at www.packardclub.org.

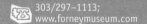
and Packard. There are examples of many rare makes, and unusual celebrity cars, such as Amelia Earhart's bright yellow Kissel and an eye-catching Rolls Royce Phantom I once owned by billionaire Prince Aly Kahn. The antique bikes and trikes are interesting, especially the hiwheel bicycle—the type with the giant wheel in the front and the tiny one in the rear. You have to wonder how anyone ever learned to ride one, at least without getting pretty bashed up in the process (perhaps a good place to mention the benefits of bicycle helmets!).

The museum is primarily a look-but-don't-touch establishment, though kids are permitted to climb up on one of the locomotives. It's hard to get them back off it once they do.

KEEP IN MIND
The Forney Museum's large gift shop is a definite draw, with toys, lots of models, books, and all kinds of transportation novelty items. Be prepared for kids to want to go there and to buy something. There's a good range of prices, though.

EATS FOR KIDS This is an industrial area, so for dining head back downtown. Try **BD's Mongolian Barbecue** (1620 Wazee, tel. 303/571–1824), where you can pick out the items you want grilled (meats, fish, vegetables), and the sauce and spices you want with them. Watch it all cooked up in front of you, then enjoy. The kids deal ($4.99) gives children the same choices for a slightly cheaper price. **Rocky Mountain Diner** (800 18th St., tel. 303/293–8383) has typical diner food. For kids there are corn dogs, chicken, and macaroni and cheese, among other things ($3.99).

THE FORT

I t's a restaurant. It's a re-created fort. It's the setting for historical reenactments, powwows, and more. Owner Sam Arnold based the design of his establishment on an old drawing he found of Bent's Fort, a major fur trading center on the Santa Fe Trail in the 1830s. To maintain historical accuracy, Arnold and his family helped make 80,000 mud and straw adobe bricks to construct the building.

The nonprofit Tesoro Foundation, created by the Arnolds to preserve the culture of Colorado's past, stages a variety of family events at the Fort. Among them are an April Powwow with Native American performers and up to 10,000 visitors, and an October Encampment where more than a dozen interpreters reenact the daily life of mountain men, trappers, and traders. At the Encampment, kids can pull taffy (just as it was done at Bent's Fort), and everyone can learn traditional dances. Each November families gather for "The Night the Stars Fell," a reference to the Leonid Meteor Shower of

KEEP IN MIND The Tesoro Foundation was created in 2001, and it's now rapidly growing and expanding. Many more events are planned at The Fort and other venues, and the foundation is actively working with local school districts. For the most current information, go to www.tesorofoundation.org.

HEY, KIDS! Back in the old days, buildings were made of some pretty strange materials—like ox blood. When you go to the Fort, look at the ground in the St. Vrain Bar. Underneath the wood planks you can see a dirt floor. That floor was made the same way many were in the 1800s—with a traditional mixture of earth and ox blood. It was covered with the wood planks you see there now because the restaurant owners soon found out that women's high heels and the earthen floors "were not compatible."

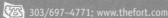
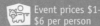
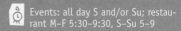

1833, when 150,000 meteors swooshed through the sky. The Denver Astronomical Society explains the science and provides telescopes, while storytellers offer a historical perspective. June through August, a historical music series under the stars brings the instruments and genres of the past to life. Interpreters lead educational walk-throughs of The Fort about once a month.

The Fort features historically accurate cuisine (for those dying to try Rocky Mountain oysters, here's your chance). Like champagne? They open the bottles by tomahawk here. And you'll want to learn the Mountain Man's toast (which works equally well with soda pop), so you can join in when he stops by your table: "Here's to the childs what's come afore, and here's to the pilgrims what's come arter. May yer trails be free of grizzlies, your packs filled with plews, and may you have fat buffler in your pot. *Waugh!*" Sounds good— but what are plews, anyway?

EATS FOR KIDS The Fort is famous for its excellent game and other grilled meats and fish, as well as some nongrilled entrées. Not surprisingly, the kids' menu falls along the same lines, offering such exotic entrées as grilled buffalo burger, elk steak, and buffalo prime rib. For less adventurous eaters, there's also fried chicken breast and beef prime rib. Like the adult menu, the children's menu is relatively pricey ($6.95–$14.95). There are outdoor food stands on event days.

FOUR MILE HISTORIC PARK

our miles from downtown Denver, this 12-acre site along the banks of Cherry Creek is one of the best places to learn about Colorado history, because it is a microcosm of development in Denver from the 1850s to the 1880s. The original log home here was built in about 1859 by the Brantner brothers. Mary Cawker bought it in 1860 and, with the help of her two teenaged children, ran it as a stage stop on the Cherokee Trail. After the devastating Cherry Creek flood of 1864, Cawker sold the house and surrounding 160 acres to Levi and Millie Booth, who continued to run the place as a stage stop until the railroad reached Denver in 1870. It was the Booths who built the brick addition and moved an 1860s frame house to the property, creating the U-shape home you see today.

Visitors can stroll around the living-history homestead on their own; kids love seeing the goats and chickens on the property, but it's the massive Percheron draft horses that really get their attention. Do take a guided tour of the house as well. The log portion is Denver's

EATS FOR KIDS **Sam Taylor's Bar-B-Q** (435 S. Cherry, tel. 303/388–9300), at Cherry and Leetsdale, is considered by many aficionados to be the best place for barbecue in town. Decide for yourself. It's not far from the historic park, it's totally casual, and you can sit at picnic tables outside. Barbecue sandwiches and dinners are moderately priced. The kids' menu offerings range from hot dogs and barbecued pork and beef sandwiches to catfish and ribs ($2.75–$5.75).

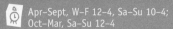

oldest standing structure and depicts the world of the early pioneers. The brick addition is a visual reminder of how lifestyles changed as owners became wealthier and as the railroad made it possible to acquire more fashionable furnishings.

The park hosts many special events, mostly in summer. During Westward Ho!, for example, families panned for gold, played games, and sang songs typical of 140 years ago. Sometimes there are living-history demonstrations, such as blacksmithing and butter churning. Most major holidays are celebrated with historical activities, and on weekends, weather permitting, you can climb aboard a stagecoach for a ride around the property and on part of the Cherokee Trail. (Imagine traveling cross-country that way!) Concerts in the shady grove are a fine way to spend a summer evening; call ahead to find out when they're scheduled.

HEY, KIDS! Four Mile House got its name because it was, yep, 4 miles from the city of Denver (present-day downtown). Back when it was a stagecoach stop, it took two hours to get there from Denver by stage. Today you can make the drive in 20 minutes.

KEEP IN MIND When you sign up for the guided tour of the house, ask about Family Activity Packs, which are included with the tour price. Take the pack with you as you explore, making all of the suggested stops. Pan for gold on Cherry Creek, pull water from the farm well and "wash" laundry on scrub boards, visit the Plains Indian tepee and learn about the Cheyenne and Arapahoe people, and play the Cherokee Trail Game where you read about and solve problems that would have come up for travelers on the trail.

GEORGETOWN LOOP RAILROAD

Sure, you can zip from Georgetown to Silver Plume on Interstate 70 in a few minutes—the two mountain towns are just two miles apart. So why spend 1 hour and 10 minutes riding the train? Because kids love trains, the view from the windows is spectacular, it's a ride right out of Colorado's mining and railroad history, and you get a firsthand look at a masterpiece of engineering. If that's not enough, the 4½ miles of twisting track is a thrill.

Georgetown, 42 miles west of Denver on I–70, was reached by railroad in 1877. Continuing the tracks to Silver Plume, only two miles away but 600 feet higher in elevation, proved a daunting challenge. In order to make the climb, the tracks had to spiral around two-and-a-half times. At the narrowest part of the valley, a 300-foot-long, nearly 100-foot high viaduct was built so the track could loop over itself—the most complex railroad loop in the world. With such remarkable engineering and stunning scenery, the

EATS FOR KIDS The **Happy Cooker** (in Georgetown, 303/569–3166) serves breakfast and lunch all day. Everything is made from scratch and delicious, but most popular are the waffles, breads, and soups ($3.75–$8). There's no kids' menu, but kids can order half portions.

HEY, KIDS! The Georgetown Loop is a narrow-gauge railroad, meaning the rails are 3 feet apart. Standard gauge tracks are 4 feet, 8½ inches apart. Why was narrow-gauge better in the mountains? Think money! Although the difference between the two gauges is less than two feet, the cost difference was huge stretched over many miles. Plus, narrow-gauge equipment is smaller and can climb steeper grades and negotiate tighter curves (count the hairpin turns on the Georgetown Loop). That, too, meant lower construction costs—and made it possible to build one very cool railway line.

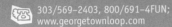

railroad became a turn-of-the-century tourist attraction. Yet even that couldn't save it when the rise of the automobile and collapse of the mining industry rendered the railroad obsolete. Track and bridges were dismantled and sold for scrap, which might have meant the permanent demise of the railway, were it not for the efforts of the Colorado Historical Society. Today's Devil Gate Viaduct was dedicated in 1984, 100 years after the original was built, and the Georgetown Loop Railroad is again one of Colorado's great tourist—and family—attractions.

You can depart on the round-trip ride from Georgetown or Silver Plume; the train leaves approximately every hour and twenty minutes. Either way, take the time to add on a tour of the Lebanon Silver Mine, reachable only by train. With Historical Society guides leading the way, you'll see and feel what it was like to be a hard rock miner—then hop back on the train to finish your trip.

KEEP IN MIND If you plan on touring Lebanon Mine, remember that it's a walking tour that lasts almost an hour and a half, requiring good walking shoes. And no matter how hot it is outside, the mine is a constant 44° F, so bring a sweater or jacket for everyone. The mine tour is available on all departures except the last trip of the day from both Silver Plume and Georgetown. You can get off at the mine going either direction, but you can only make reservations from Silver Plume.

GRIZZLY ROSE

Looking for a real Western boot stompin' good ol' time? Head to the Grizzly Rose. Sunday is Family Night at the Grizz, so kids of all ages are welcome to come on in and kick up their heels. Some of the greatest names in country and western music have played here, from Willie Nelson to Faith Hill to Garth Brooks, and no doubt some of the unknown bands that make a Sunday appearance will one day be household names, too. If you're lucky you can say you saw them way back when.

This is a huge place—40,000 square feet to be exact. Those who want to sit will find plenty of tables and chairs, most with good views of the dance floor and stage. The upper seating area is a little quieter than the main area, so if you're thinking of indulging in conversation, that's the best choice. But why sit down? There's a pool hall, a video arcade, and a way big dance floor on which to practice your two-step. (Alas, there are no dance

HEY, KIDS! The Grizz is famous for its Western dancing, especially line dancing. Don't be embarrassed if you don't know how to do it. Just get out there on the dance floor and join all the other kids. One nice part is you don't have to have a partner or wait for someone else to ask you! You just get out on the floor and join the crowd. If you've never done it, stand behind one of the kids who knows the steps and follow along. By the end of a song or two, you'll be surprised just how well you're doing.

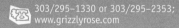5450 N. Valley Hwy., North Denver

$5 ages 12 and up

303/295-1330 or 303/295-2353;
www.grizzlyrose.com

Su 6 PM–11 PM

All, but especially teens

lessons on Sunday night.) If you want to get your boots shined or your hat shaped, you can do that, too, or buy some new duds at the Double Bar K Store. Rodeo rider wannabes will head for the mechanical bull—which is slowed way down for kids whether they ride with a parent or on their own. (Anyone under age 18 must have a parent's consent before climbing on.)

Although even young children will find much to like here, this is a place that's especially popular with teens, and you'll see a lot of 15- to 18-year-olds on Sunday nights. Teens of that age often roll their eyes at the suggestion of spending an evening out with the family, but here's an option that both teens and parents can cotton to.

EATS FOR KIDS
The Grizzly Rose's own **Chuckwagon Café** is extremely casual, serving typical down-home Western food. Don't expect anything fancy—like tablecloths, for example. Appetizers include chicken wings, and there are burgers, brisket, and Mexican dishes among the main courses (about $3–$7).

KEEP IN MIND Although Sunday night is family night, all guests under the age of 18 must leave by 11 PM. The truth is you'll probably want to leave earlier than that, because starting at about 9:30 or 10 the Grizz tends to get very crowded and very smoky. Families with young children usually arrive when the doors open at 6 and leave by about 8:30 or 9:00. After that time, the place gets pretty packed with teens; if you have adolescents, that may be when they most want to make an appearance.

GUNSLINGERS, GHOSTS & GOLD WALKING TOUR

Dee Chandler and Beaux Blakemore are Certified Paranormal Investigators and Ghost Hunters, which may be why their only-slightly-scary-but-fiendishly-fascinating tour was voted one of the Denver's best attractions. There are two routes to choose from, LoDo (Lower Downtown) or Uptown. LoDo is better for younger kids. Either is about a 1½-mile, two-hour trek on which you'll learn about colorful characters from the city's rough-and-tumble past, many of whom apparently remain today as the occasional apparitions in some of the city's historic buildings—no shock for any kid who loves the *X-Files*.

Chandler and Blakemore know about more than ghosts. They regale you with stories of gun-toting gamblers, rags-to-riches-to-rags miners (such as Horace Tabor, one of Denver's most famous citizens, a boom-and-buster whose divorce and remarriage scandalized the city), and infamous outlaws, including Doc Holliday. In fact, Denver apparently is only a middling ghost-ridden city—New Orleans and Chicago are far wealthier in haunts.

HEY, KIDS!
Stump your friends with trivia you've learned on the tour, such as: whose body was kept on ice and under armed guard for five months before finally being buried—and why? How did "Wheelbarrow" McGraw earn his nickname? Why was Billy known as "The Kid"?

EATS FOR KIDS   You stop at **Josephina's** (1433 Larimer St., tel. 303/623–0166) for a soda break on the LoDo tour, and it's a good choice for a meal, too. You'll find all the normal Italian favorites, including excellent pizza. In summer, if you don't want to stay inside (where ghosts of a mother and daughter are said to linger, the tragic result of a father hiring a hitman to off his daughter's boyfriend), ask for a sidewalk table. Ghosts aside, Denver families have been coming here for years for the cool atmosphere, historic downtown location, live jazz, people-watching, and moderate prices.

Box 481136

 303/860-8687;
www.denverhauntedhistory.com

 $15 ages 13 and up,
$7.50 ages 7–12

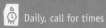 Daily, call for times

 7 and up

As far as families are concerned, that's a plus, because the tour isn't likely to cause sleepless nights (though even nonscary ghosts may bother certain kids, something to consider before signing up). The guides know a wealth of information, which they share liberally, and all tours are historically accurate—even if folks at the Denver Mint deny that they've ever been robbed. (You'll know better by the end of the tour.) In fact, one of the best features of the tour is that while it's 100 percent entertaining, it's also a mini-history class— proof that education and fun aren't mutually exclusive.

For those with potentially tired legs, there is a soda (or cocktail) break during the tour— in a haunted building, naturally. The LoDo tour starts at 18th and Wynkoop and ends at 19th and Blake; Uptown starts at 14th and Larimer and ends at 17th and Market. The company also has a one-hour tour, less-than-a-mile tour of Morrison, which boasts its own ghosts and gunslingers.

KEEP IN MIND Parents should know that some LoDo tours meander in the last 10 minutes through the former red light district, and that stories there center around one or two characters and ghosts who worked in what would be considered less than upstanding circumstances. If this is a problem for your group, consider the Sunday afternoon outing, which generally bypasses that once seedy side of town. You can also request a totally G-rated tour on other days; the tour operators will do their best to accommodate you.

HYLAND HILLS WATER WORLD

Water World is a 64-acre aquatic amusement park with lots of wet fun and big-time thrills. If your kids are young and you're not in the mood for agitation, you might head for the mild Lazy River or one of the wave pools, where you can relax and splash and play. Families with preschoolers may never leave Wally World, where minislides and shallow pools are designed for the very young. (Grown-ups are allowed on the small slides only with a tot in tow.) But if you're looking for more action, there are plenty of options.

Some rides the whole family can do together: the Ragin' Colorado is ¾ mile of simulated white-water rafting; Lost River of the Pharoahs and Voyage to the Center of the Earth are theme rides that will scare some young kids and delight others with cobras and "molten lava" (Pharoahs), and dinosaurs (Earth). Thrill Hill is a perfect parent–child ride consisting of four moderately steep body slides, including Tandemonium with twists and turns for two. Teens and other thrill-seekers should check out Bermuda Triangle and Screamin' Mimi, both steep, fast slides. Prank Tank over in the Fun House area spits sliders from a steep

KEEP IN MIND Some additional expenditures here are worthwhile. (You can make up the cost by purchasing discounted tickets on-line.) Get an all-day locker ($8); other lockers are just 50¢, but you pay each time you open them. Rent tubes ($4); you avoid long pick-up lines at the attractions requiring tubes, and kids love playing with them in the pools. Consider life jackets; they're provided but require a deposit. All kids age 3 and under must be in swim diapers, available through Water World. You can't bring your own water wings, floats, or tubes, and no alcohol or glass is permitted.

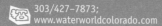
1800 W. 89th Ave., Federal Heights

303/427-7873;
www.waterworldcolorado.com

$24.95 ages 14
and up, $20.95
ages 4–12

Last weekend in May to Labor Day,
10–6

All ages

chute into circular bowls where they spin until reaching a pool. Space Bowl takes that concept one step farther by enclosing the chute and bowl so that you slide and spin in total darkness. (Sound like fun?) Zoomerang is the half-pipe of the pool world: it's four stories high and if you think you'll keep your stomach on the way down, think again. And even more slides await those with nerves of steel. (Some do have height requirements.)

This is a big place, and it can get crowded, so make sure kids know not to wander off. Once you settle into an area, pick a nearby spot to meet in case anyone gets separated from the group.

On-line tickets are discounted. All-day lockers $8, including $5 deposit; Tube rentals: $4 for one, $12.50 for the Float-for-Less package where you pay for three and get a fourth tube free.

HEY, KIDS! Here are some Water World Fast Stats: you slide 30 mph on Screamin' Mimi, drop 60 feet in three seconds on Bermuda Triangle, and race 40 mph on Pipeline, Red Line, and Flat Line. Red Line is eight stories high, Zoomerang is four. Yikes!

EATS FOR KIDS Once you get here you're here, but there are plenty of places to eat. **Big Mike's** old-fashioned diner, **Pier 1 Pizza, Taco Wally's, Key Largo Café,** and **Boardwalk Foods** are among the choices. Key Largo has made-to-order burgers and Pier 1 has fresh-baked pizzas. Grilled chicken sandwiches are available in a couple of the restaurants, and Taco Wally's is, of course, Mexican food. A lot of the food is downright decent, and it's reasonably priced. The average charge for a burger, fries, and pop is about $5.

JUNGLEQUEST

Take the kids to the Jungle and let them meet adventure head on. Maybe they'll want to challenge themselves on the 22-foot climbing wall or the 50-foot bouldering wall. Or maybe they'll want to zip full tilt through the Tyrolean Traverse or cross mighty gulfs on rope bridges. There are caves, ziplines, and other activities galore in this indoor adventure center—if this place doesn't tire them out, nothing will.

But that's not what Junglequest all about. Sure, it's fun, but it's not just your average indoor amusement center. It's designed to make kids feel good about testing their limits and meeting challenges—in a safe environment. It's designed to help them succeed, even if they're a little reluctant. A lot of that has to do with the people in charge. Owner Doug Root has a degree in recreation administration and business, and he bought Junglequest because it was a business his family could love, and one that had potential to be an

KEEP IN MIND Junglequest welcomes all kids, including those with special needs. If your child has special physical, mental, or emotional needs, talk to the directors about it. They will develop an individualized program tailored to your child, one that's fun, challenging, and rewarding.

HEY, KIDS! Girl Scouts and Boy Scouts can earn badges at Junglequest. If you're a Boy Scout you can earn the Climbing Merit Badge. Instructors will guide you through a curriculum in which you'll find out how to tie knots, belay, and rappel. You'll also learn about safety, and, most important, trust. Girl Scouts can earn the High Adventure Merit Badge. You'll learn how to be a challenge course assistant, how to navigate the course, and all about course safety systems. Instructors will even talk to you about career options.

8000 S. Lincoln St., Littleton

 M–Th 7 AM–7 PM, F–Sa 7 AM–8 PM

$10 for the first 1½ hours, $3 each additional ½ hour

303/738-9844; www.junglequest.net

5 and up

important resource in the community. The program director has an MS in education and a BS in therapeutic recreation; he's also certified in first aid, CPR, and wilderness education. The program coordinator has a degree in recreation, and other staff members have or are working on degrees in related fields. As a result, this is a place where the staff is attuned to learning, fun, and safety—the very things you'd want for your kids in an activity program. It's not surprising that Junglequest won the 2000 Blue Chip Enterprise Award from the U.S. Chamber of Commerce.

Of course kids don't care much about that—but they like that they can get one-on-one training on the climbing wall. Kids and parents will both like that there are summer and winter day camps lasting a day, a week, or an entire vacation break.

EATS FOR KIDS **Old Chicago** (7961 S. Broadway, Littleton, tel. 303/794–5959) is a decent chain just across the street. Kids can choose pizza, spaghetti, corn dog, hamburger, or chicken fingers, with pop ($2.99). **Gunther Toody's,** a '50s-style diner, is fun. Locations include Littleton at Wadsworth and Bowles (tel. 303/932–1957), Englewood at Arapahoe near I-25 (tel. 303/799–1958), and Glendale at Alameda and Leetsdale (tel. 303/399–1959). Call just to hear them answer the phone: "Howdy doody, Gunther Toody's, what's shakin'?" Eats for kids include pasta, burgers, grilled cheese, and hot dogs. The meal comes with pop and a sundae ($3.80).

LARIMER SQUARE

What's great about Larimer Square is that it's a place where families can still stroll through history. You can visit just to walk around and look at the old buildings—Larimer Square is listed on the National Register of Historic Places—to shop, eat, or attend one of the many special events held there. Oktoberfest, Winterfest, and the Summer Night Concert Series are all popular with families.

When you look at gentrified, quaint Larimer Square today, it's hard to believe that it was once Denver's most disreputable neighborhood—the place where gun-toting gamblers, drifters, and assorted outlaws and con men congregated in the saloons and gambling halls. Houses of ill-repute rounded out the neighborhood. Larimer is, in fact, Denver's oldest street. The city's very first structures were built on this site but were destroyed in the fire of 1863. Today Larimer has been refurbished, with gas lamps that light up its fine Victorian woodwork and architecture. You can take an old-fashioned carriage ride if

HEY, KIDS! Larimer was once the wildest street in Denver, where famous and not-so-famous outlaws often roamed. Of them all, Soapy Smith may have been the most colorful character. He earned his nickname by selling soap on Larimer Street. He'd pretend to insert folded dollar bills under the wrappers of random bars in order to entice people to buy. A total schemer, he finally entered politics and was run out of town after rigging elections. He met his demise in Skagway, Alaska, where, as one historian put it, "a public-minded citizen shot and killed him."

you don't want to explore on foot or bike—but do make a point to walk around a bit. Pick up one of the walking tour brochures, available at most of the shops. It identifies the location and history of the original settlement and provides background about the existing buildings.

There are some Larimer Square shops that kids will enjoy checking out, like Iconoclast Motorcycles and Earthzone with its minerals, gems, and fossils. Blazing Saddles (tel. 303/534–5255) is a bike rental company that has children's bikes available. You can pick up rentals there and head across the street to the bike path to explore. Denver's approximately 150 miles of paved bike paths allow you the option of a short ride or a long one, depending on the ages of your kids and your interest.

KEEP IN MIND Much of Larimer's colorful past involves Denver's famous madams and houses of ill-repute—something to share with kids as you see fit. For a good history of Denver, log onto www.denvergov.org; click on "history" in the welcome area.

EATS FOR KIDS **Josephina's** (tel. 303/623–0166) is a great Italian restaurant complete with a ghost (see Gunslingers, Ghosts & Gold Walking Tour, #25). **Tommy Tsunami's** (tel. 303/534–5050) has kid and adult favorites such as Teriyaki chicken or beef, stir fries, and noodle bowls. If you don't want a full meal, grab a smoothie to walk with at **Jamba Juice** (tel. 303/607–0019) or go to **Josh & John's** (tel. 303/628–0310) for its locally famous homemade ice cream. Most restaurants are open until 10 PM or later, depending on the night.

LEANIN' TREE MUSEUM

You might recognize the Leanin' Tree name from cowboy Christmas cards and other Western greeting cards sold worldwide. The museum, located on the outskirts of Boulder, is a happy offshoot of the greeting card company, for as owner Edward P. Trumble traveled in search of art for his cards, he had the chance to become acquainted with virtually every major Western artist to come down the pike in the past 40 years. In doing so, he put together one of the country's largest and most impressive collections of post-1950 fine art of the American West. The museum houses his collection and is essentially his gift to the public—admission is always free.

Leanin' Tree has been called Colorado's best small museum, and once you go you'll know why. On display are nearly 300 paintings and 85 major bronze sculptures, and you don't have to be an expert in Western art to enjoy them. Although the museum isn't specifically

KEEP IN MIND The "Can You Find?" list does more than make wandering the museum fun—though it certainly does that. It also encourages children to slow down and look carefully at the details of the artwork. Who knows? They may even see some things you miss!

HEY, KIDS! Ask at the front desk for a "Can You Find?" list. On it will be 20 to 24 objects to search for in the paintings and sculptures around the museum. Some of the objects are ordinary—a chair, a tractor, a sailboat. Others are unusual by today's standards; when was the last time you saw bear claws or someone with a gold tooth? Keep your eyes open—you never know where you might find one of the objects. But don't worry too much about finding everyone; you get a prize just for trying.

 6055 Longbow Dr., Boulder

 Free

303/530–1442;
www.leanintree.com

 M–F 8–4:30, Sa–Su 10–4

 6 and up

geared to children, parents usually find that their kids are naturally drawn to this eminently accessible artistic genre, with its images of cowboys and Indians, bucking broncos, spotted ponies, and Western wildlife. Children have often learned about pioneers and other aspects of America's Western expansion in school, and they recognize these themes in the vibrant artwork. (It's no surprise that the museum regularly welcomes groups of local school children, and that as a field trip it gets rave reviews.) Some of the pieces capture a colorful and, for the most part, long-gone way of life, while others offer an artist's enduring vision of rugged Western landscapes that have remained little changed over centuries.

Although there's plenty here to linger over, the museum is small enough not to be overwhelming, and it doesn't require a huge investment of time—a benefit parents of younger children in particular can appreciate.

EATS FOR KIDS There's nothing by the museum, so drive back into Boulder proper. If you've been at the museum until late in the afternoon on a Sunday, try **Jose Muldoon's** *(see #11)*—kids eat free (with paying adult) on Sunday at Jose's. Or head over to the Pearl Street Mall and go Japanese at **Japango** (1136 Pearl St., tel. 303/938–0330). Kids can choose teriyaki, sushi, Japanese chicken nuggets, or croquettes ($5.95). Some dishes are served in wooden boats.

LOOKOUT MOUNTAIN NATURE CENTER

In the Nature Center, part of the 110-acre Lookout Mountain Nature Preserve (which in turn is part of the Jefferson County Open Space), families will find interactive exhibits and programs designed to "reveal some of nature's secrets." Younger kids will probably be interested in opportunities to examine real mountain lion claws or to feel the different furs of a bear, lion, deer, and fox. And having the chance to practice using binoculars and listening devices is always a hit. The building itself is also of interest because it's what's known as a "sustainable design," meaning it was built using recycled, reused, and Earth-friendly materials. These are labeled throughout the center, and you can fill in the "sustainable design bingo" card as you walk around and spot those features.

If the weather is good, families should plan on spending time outdoors in the preserve, too. There are 1½ miles of gently rolling walking trails along which you might spot Colorado wildlife; even if you don't, it's nice to walk on trails even toddlers can manage, and there are always discoveries to be made simply watching insects or looking under trailside rocks.

HEY, KIDS! Do birds walk upside down? The Pygmy nuthatch does (listen for its "peep, peep, peep" call), but that's not what researchers find most interesting. This little nuthatch is called a "keystone" species because its presence and health is an indication of the health of the whole ponderosa pine forest. While you're exploring the preserve, also look for Abert's squirrels. They're usually black and have long hair tufts on their ears. The only place these critters live is in ponderosa pine forests and their *only* food is parts of the ponderosa pine tree. Imagine eating only spaghetti every day of your life!

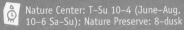 910 Colorow Rd., Golden

 Free; donations accepted

 Nature Center: T–Su 10–4 (June–Aug, 10–6 Sa–Su); Nature Preserve: 8–dusk

 303/526-0594

2 and up

You won't be lacking for photo ops, either: on a clear day you can see Pikes Peak rising in the distance. Families who love to hike and those with older kids may want to make a day of it, connecting from the preserve trails to trails in Apex and Windy Saddle parks, Beaver Brook Trail, or even up to Buffalo Bill's Museum and Grave.

Throughout the year the center and preserve host a variety of special guided programs (mostly free). Typical are the Budding Naturalist series, for which kids get a Discovery Pack filled with fun things to help them explore and better understand the world outside, and Blooming and Buzzing, in which families search with naturalists for native wildflowers and their buzzing "partners."

EATS FOR KIDS

The center has five picnic tables; if you're hiking and the weather is nice, plan to picnic. Or eat in Golden at **Woody's Woodfired Pizza & Watering Hole** (1305 Washington Ave., tel. 303/277–0443), where the buffet includes pizza, soup, and salad ($3.99 kids, $7.50 adults).

KEEP IN MIND Program schedules listing activities at Lookout Mountain Nature Center (and other county parks) use an icon system to denote age appropriateness of the various offerings. Those marked with a star are for ages 2–5 with an adult; a butterfly indicates that the program is for ages 6–10 with an adult. Programs marked with a magnifying glass are for adults and adolescents at least 13 years old. A telescope denotes activities for individuals and families with children age 10 and older, while a bear paw means the program is for individuals and families with kids age 2 and up.

MOLLY BROWN HOUSE MUSEUM

She was never called Molly during her lifetime (she was Maggie), but her flair and zest for life made her one of Colorado's best-known historical figures. Her life and story became the stuff of legend in the Broadway musical the *Unsinkable Molly Brown*, but today's children may be more aware of her from the cinema extravaganza about the sinking of the *Titanic* (which she survived). It's that connection that makes this tour especially interesting to kids, though Molly's house was one of Denver's most popular attractions long before the movie.

The distinctive lava stone and sandstone house, its entry guarded by impressive stone lions, was built in 1889 by one of Denver's premier architects, William Lang, and it's a Victorian masterpiece, complete with the velvet, lace, and polished wood you would expect. It was purchased by Molly's husband, J. J. Brown, in 1894 after he hit pay dirt with his Little Johnny gold mine in Leadville. Not all of the furnishings were once owned by

EATS FOR KIDS Two doors away from the Molly Brown House is **Chipotle Mexican Grill** (1300 Pennsylvania, tel. 303/831–8831). It's a chain and more faux than real Mexican, but the food—burritos, tacos, etc.— is decent and plentiful and the mood is family casual ($5 or $6).

HEY, KIDS! Lots of stories are told about Molly Brown. There's the one about the floors of her Leadville home being inlaid with silver dollars, and another about a $300,000 mining payroll that went up in smoke after Molly put it in the wood stove for safekeeping. One of the wildest has her rescued from a raft on the Mississippi by Mark Twain after a cyclone. And then there are the tales of her bravery and heroism the night the *Titanic* went down in icy northern seas. Which ones are true? Find out on the tour.

1340 Pennsylvania Ave., Downtown

 303/832–4092;
www.mollybrown.org

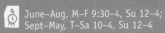 $6.50 ages 13 and
up, $2.50 ages 6–12

 June–Aug, M–F 9:30–4, Su 12–4;
Sept–May, T–Sa 10–4, Su 12–4

8 and up

the Browns, but many of their personal belongings can be seen in the three-story home. The Browns actually weren't here that often, for they spent much of their newfound wealth traveling the world, leasing the house to various prominent citizens. It was even the governor's mansion for a year.

The house remained in Molly's name until her death in 1932, after which it was sold and frequently remodeled. A historical foundation bought it in the 1970s and meticulously restored it to its present Victorian elegance. Tours last about 30 minutes and are led by women dressed in turn-of-the-20th-century costumes who love to tell visitors about the *real* Molly Brown, as opposed to the fictional character of stage and film. The real Molly doesn't disappoint, for she was outspoken, courageous, and a feminist long before the term was even used. Her rags-to-riches rise to fame is quintessential Americana.

KEEP IN MIND Throughout the year the museum has special events—most of which you must reserve for well ahead of time, because they fill up fast. In October the house is decorated with spiders, ghosts, and witches' hats for a Halloween Tea. Older kids and teens might like October's Victorian Horrors, during which actors impersonate the likes of Edgar Allan Poe, Mary Shelley, and H. G. Wells while reading from the authors' creepy classics. There are several Holiday High Teas in December. Check the Web site for listings. If your kids enjoy *Titanic* souvenirs, they'll find much to like in the gift shop.

NATIONAL CENTER FOR ATMOSPHERIC RESEARCH (NCAR)

18

N CAR was established in 1960 as a center for research on atmospheric and related science problems. Sounds like heady stuff for little guys, but NCAR is one cool place for all ages. To begin with, some of the interactive science displays were designed at Exploratorium in San Francisco, arguably one of the best science museums in the country.

At NCAR visitors learn about the work real researchers are conducting right there at the center, and about the processes that dictate weather and climate. Children of different ages will get something different out of the experience, but every visitor, even a toddler, is likely to learn something and have fun doing it. Very young children like the hands-on weather machines that simulate tornadoes, lightning, and more. If your kids have ever asked the age-old question "Why is the sky blue?" point them in the direction of the Blue Sky Exhibit. There's often a free tour starting at noon, and parents with school-

HEY, KIDS! Looking for science on the Web? The cool folks at NCAR recommend Windows to the Universe, www.windows.ucar.edu, a space and science site, and NASA's starchild.gsfc.nasa.gov. There's an interactive hurricane page in the weather section of www.athena.ivv.gov. You can also log on to NCAR's Web site, click on UCAR (it stands for University Corporation for Atmospheric Research), click on Storm Prediction Center, then Cool Images, for pictures of awesome weather happenings, like tornadoes touching down. Click on the weather page for the latest stats on local weather (updated every five minutes) and make your own predictions.

age kids should consider joining in. It lasts about an hour, and it's one of the most popular tours for local school children, so guides are adept at making the information not only accessible but fascinating, and they never mind questions. The center suggests this tour even for preschoolers, and some do fine with it. Consider the staying power of your child before committing, or simply be prepared to duck out if there's a problem.

You're welcome to do your own self-guided tour, too, and there's plenty of literature at the various exhibits to help explain the science. Whether you explore with a guide or on your own, start with the brief orientation film. There's something scientific for everyone in the store, a veritable treasure chest of cool toys, books, and other fun stuff. It's all educational, but you don't have to tell the kids.

KEEP IN MIND Wear good walking shoes and include NCAR's Weather Trail on your visit. The ⁹⁄₁₀-mile loop (wheelchair-accessible) has 11 viewpoints, each with a sign explaining a facet of the wild, varied conditions here. Hikers can also connect to Boulder Mountain Park's extensive trails from NCAR.

EATS FOR KIDS Eat with the scientists—who knows what you might learn!— at NCAR's **Foothills Lab Cafeteria.** It's open 7:30–9:30 for breakfast, 11:30–1:30 for lunch, and it may just be the best deal on meals in town. Where else can you get two eggs and bacon for $2.70 or cereal for 90¢? The lunch menu includes sandwiches ($2.50–$3.25), soup ($1.50–$1.95), and hot dishes such as enchilada casseroles and sloppy Joes ($3.85–$4.60), plus cookies and milk, a favorite with scientists young and old.

OCEAN JOURNEY

At Denver's aquarium, Ocean Journey, exhibits focus on two different rivers, from their headwaters in the mountains to their journey's end at the sea. As you follow along, you view the animals and plants that live in the rivers and along the banks, and get a sense of the natural ecosystems supported by these important waterways. The experience isn't just about sights, but about sounds and smells, too.

Not surprisingly, one of the rivers is the mighty Colorado, which travels from the Continental Divide nearly 1,500 miles to the Sea of Cortez (also called the Gulf of California). It's fascinating to see the diversity of habitats that a single river runs through (and thus has a hand in creating). In the high country the Colorado is home to graceful cutthroat trout; as part of Mexico's Sea of Cortez, it provides food and shelter for nearly 6,000 tropical fish. On the Colorado visitors find the fossilized remains of a marine reptile and experience the force of a flash flood.

EATS FOR KIDS At **The Market** (1445 Larimer, tel. 303/534–5140), a grocery, deli, and restaurant, people shop, take out food, and sit down to eat. You can get deli sandwiches all day and into the night, as well as soups, pasta salads, and more.

HEY, KIDS! Aquariums usually have only fish and marine animals on exhibit. No other aquarium in the whole world has tigers, so why do you think this one does? One reason is that Sumatran tigers really love the water. They spend hours swimming in the river because it helps them lower their body temperature and cool down in the hot, steamy jungle. But there's another reason the scientists at Ocean Journey decided to break with tradition and include land mammals in the exhibit: they wanted to show that water is essential to much more than fish. What do you think of that?

 700 Water St., Central Platte Valley

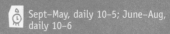 $14.95 adults, $12.95 ages 13–17, $6.95 ages 4–12

 Sept–May, daily 10–5; June–Aug, daily 10–6

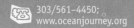 303/561–4450; www.oceanjourney.org

All ages

But what is a Sumatran tiger doing at a Denver aquarium? Hunkering down on the banks of the second replica river, the Kampar, which runs from the volcanic Barisan Mountains on the island of Sumatra down to the South China Sea. The Indonesian River Journey exhibit includes rain forests and more than 3,000 exotic fish, including a variety of sharks and the odd Napoleon wrasse. Ocean Journey visitors "travel" over, under, around, and through rivers, coral reefs, and deep ocean environments, seeing fish and water from all different perspectives. If you've ever wanted a fish's-eye view of the world, this is the place to find it. In 2001 the aquarium added Seafoam Fun Zone, a play area for young children, and a motion simulator to take older kids, teens, and adults on a variety of interactive rides, such as Shark Island and Sub Race.

As of March 2002 it seems likely that Ocean Journey will soon close. Call ahead before you plan a visit.

KEEP IN MIND The aquarium isn't huge; you can cover it in an hour and a half or so. It's also better suited to young children than to pre-teens and teens. What's good about that is that the Children's Museum of Denver (see #53) is near by, and visits to both can make for a fun day out with the kids. In fact, you can leave your car at one and hop on the trolley that runs between the two facilities to visit the other.

OUTDOOR FILM FESTIVAL

Remember when movies were actually fun for the whole family to go to? Well, you can still see family classics on the big screen in Boulder and Denver, and the best part is, you get to do it outdoors.

Come summertime, on Saturday nights (and a few Fridays) families congregate in a parking lot behind Boulder's Museum of Contemporary Art to watch movies of yesteryear. It's a BYOS affair (bring your own seating), so patrons come with lawn chairs and blankets to stake out a spot. Some of them choose more eccentric seating, to say nothing of distinctly weird dress. That's because this is an interactive theater experience, à la the *Rocky Horror Picture Show*—but family-style. An Applause-O-Meter is used to determine winners of contests for the most unusual seating (boats, sod, and your great-aunt Gladys' chintz sofa have all taken part) and best or wackiest costume. While you watch the movies, appropriate crowd reactions are encouraged. Don't expect to find anyone shushing a neighbor here.

HEY, KIDS! On the outdoor movie Web site you can vote for the movies you want to see. On one or two dates each season there are two possible movies listed. Fans simply click to vote for their favorite. In 2001, for example, you could choose between *Toy Story* and *Toy Story 2*, and between Hitchcock's *Rear Window* and *North by Northwest*. With choices like that you can't really lose, especially when you're watching out under the stars as part of a fun-loving crowd.

Boulder: 1750 13th St., parking lot between Arapahoe and Canyon; Cherry Creek: Fillmore Street between 1st and 2nd Aves.

Boulder: $5 donation requested; Cherry Creek: free

June–Sept, Boulder Sa (some F), Cherry Creek Th; gates open at 7, film at dusk (8:30–9)

www.outdoorcinema.com

All ages

In between reels there's usually some sort of off-the-wall entertainment (the Applause-O-Meter gets plenty of use), so kids have a chance to get up, run around a bit, and laugh. It's all in the spirit of good, clean fun, so grab your spare bathtub and claim your place in the parking lot. You just might win a prize.

It's a little classier Thursday nights at Fillmore Plaza in Denver (as befits the upscale North Cherry Creek neighborhood). Clowns and jugglers entertain before top family films, and lawn chairs are available for rent. Movies at both places range from age-old classics such as *To Kill a Mockingbird* and the *Wizard of Oz* to more recent favorites like *Babe* and *A Bug's Life*. *Yellow Submarine, Young Frankenstein, Pee-wee's Big Adventure,* and *Field of Dreams* have all had showings, so gather the kids and join the fun.

KEEP IN MIND
Although there's always something each season for every age, not every movie is appropriate for the youngest kids. Hitchcock classics, for example, can be scary, and other favorites, such as the *Breakfast Club* and *Ferris Bueller's Day Off*, are better for preteens and older.

EATS FOR KIDS There are concession stands, but most families arrive early and picnic before the show. In Boulder, **Whole Foods** (2301 30th St., tel. 720/563–0115) is a grocery store with takeout fare. Or eat in at **Dushanbe Teahouse** (*see #66*) adjacent to the "theater." Cherry Creek's **Noodles and Company** (2360 E. 3rd Ave., tel. 303/331–6600) has moderately priced eat-in or takeout noodles dishes of all kinds, from mac & cheese to Thai chicken ($3.75–$8).

PEARL STREET MALL

The pedestrian Pearl Street Mall was created in 1977 and has been a popular place to walk, shop, eat, watch people, and be entertained ever since. On just about any night you can stroll along listening to street musicians (not all of them good) and pause to watch magic, juggling, card tricks, or maybe a trained bird hopping through a hoop of fire. Often a crowd will gather around one of the popular street entertainers, such as a rubber-muscled contortionist who folds himself into a box or the unicyclist who performs daring stunts. Most days and evenings the Balloon Man will twist balloons into whatever shapes children desire. Maybe ZIP Code Guy will show up and you can challenge him to name the town of any ZIP code you call out (few have ever stumped him). The entertainers are usually good about getting small children up front so they can see.

The wide brick walkways, grassy areas, and flower beds of the mall are lined with shops and restaurants of all kinds. The Boulder Book Store is one of the few independent book

KEEP IN MIND Looking for a memorable costume, wash-out hair dye, or haute (and oh so au courant) hippie fashions? At The Ritz (on Walnut Street), where it's always Halloween, kids are endlessly entertained trying on frightening and fantastical garb. Biggest problem? They never want to leave.

HEY, KIDS! Pearl Street was Boulder's first street. A big complaint of early citizens was that it was *always* muddy—rain and snow wouldn't drain away. One man even wrote a poem about it in the newspaper. One of the first city ordinances (1871) required that every able-bodied man contribute two days' labor each year for street improvements—or pay $4! If towns did this today, they could save millions in maintenance costs and use that money for something else. Is that a good idea? Would you help? Pearl Street was finally paved in 1918 and mud was no longer a problem.

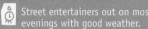

Pearl Street from 15th to 9th, Boulder

Free

Street entertainers out on most evenings with good weather.

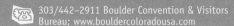
303/442-2911 Boulder Convention & Visitors Bureau; www.bouldercoloradousa.com

All ages

stores left in town, and it has an excellent children's section where kids are welcome to browse and read. The boulders in the middle of the mall south of Broadway are a hit with kids, who love to climb and slide on them. Near 15th Street are small statues of animals—a frog, a snail, a rabbit, and more—that are just right for smaller children to play on.

Throughout the year there are a variety of family-oriented festivals and musical events on the mall, and come winter it's just a couple of blocks to the ice rink. Many mall stores carry the works of local artists; the store most kids like best is Into the Wind, jam-packed with kites and every little gizmo and gadget a child could want (many costing less than a week's allowance).

EATS FOR KIDS Sooner or later everyone eats at **Freddie's Hot Dog Stand** (Pearl and Broadway). Say hi to Mike (yes, Mike, not Freddie) and get a dog for $2.25; if you're from Philly, tell him. Then walk a few feet to **Ben & Jerry's** or **Haagen-Dazs** for dessert. At **Pizza Colore,** a block east, you can get a slice or family-size pie ($1.86–$16.75). And consider one of Boulder's finest (albeit pricey) restaurants, **Dandelion** (a block south on Walnut). There's no children's menu, but the staff is child-friendly and will happily offer small portions of many dishes (which change seasonally).

PLAINS CONSERVATION CENTER

You can step back in time more than a century on a guided walk around the land and dwellings of the Plains Conservation Center. The center is all about preserving and educating—preserving 1,100 acres of short grass and mixed grass prairie and natural ecosystems, and educating people about prairie life. Pioneers who traveled west across this land would be shocked to see that so little natural prairie now remains. They would probably find it hard to believe that replicas of their humble sod dwellings, as well as Native American tepees, would be central exhibits at a center dedicated to interpreting prairie existence—human and otherwise.

The Plains Conservation Center today is entirely encircled by development, making it all the more vital as a plant and animal sanctuary and an educational tool. Standing inside a sod house, kids get a real feel for life when wood siding, let alone portable disc players, was a luxury unavailable to many. Families are welcome at public programs but must

HEY, KIDS! Calling all teens: volunteer at the Plains Conservation Center. Sure, it's work, but you'll meet interesting people and learn new skills while helping your community. Each spring, for example, the Cheyenne tepees must be set up, and teens as well as parents are invited to help. Maybe you've always wanted to be a camp counselor or are thinking about teaching school some day. You can start now learning how to work with and educate kids in the day camp. Volunteering looks great on college applications, so while you're helping others, you help yourself, too. Call the center to learn more.

 21901 E. Hampden Ave., Aurora

Programs vary; open house days free, Full Moon Walks $4, wagon rides $5

 Year-round; programs by reservation

303/693-3621; www.PlainsConservationCenter.org

3 and up

make reservations. Typical of programs are monthly Full Moon Walks on which you prowl the nighttime prairie—in the company of a knowledgeable guide—to see what can be seen. The center is home to wildlife, and depending on the time of year and your luck you might see pronghorns, jack rabbits, prairie dogs, badgers, and even rattlesnakes.

Some programs focus on the animals. In the fall there might be a Coyote Moon Walk during which you'll howl with the "moon dogs" and learn why these animals survive so successfully, even with continuing encroachment of suburbia into their habitat. You might also learn about the moon itself, or hear Cheyenne stories. Most Full Moon Walks are followed by a campfire and marshmallow roast. Other programs include open house days when you can meet the native reptiles and amphibians in the museum, and evening wagon rides.

EATS FOR KIDS
At the center there's no food for sale—nothing for sale at all, in fact. If you want to eat out before one of the public programs, your choices are limited to several fast-food places just down the road.

KEEP IN MIND If you have kids between the ages of 6 and 12, consider the center's summer Prairie Camps. There are usually two sessions with half- and full-day programs. Each day campers are challenged to live on the prairie as the pioneers and Cheyenne did, with activities in the sod village, one-room schoolhouse, and tepee village. Campers also take nature treks and wagon rides and learn about archaeology. There's usually an option at the end of each session for a Friday-night sleepover—parents are invited to stay the night, too. Camps run $50–$95 per day, sleepovers $25.

RED ROCKS AMPHITHEATER

The legendary amphitheater in Red Rocks Park, 15 miles west of Denver, opened for concerts in 1941, yet as park literature notes, it was 300 million years in the making—geologically speaking, that is. There's simply nothing else like it. Two 300-foot monoliths rise above the rock formation that is the theater. The backdrop is the front range of the Rocky Mountains, with the Continental Divide rising behind the nearby peaks and spectacular views of downtown Denver to the east.

There's no need for stage sets; the western sky turning from burnished red-gold to royal purple to a vast ceiling of stars is scenery enough. In fact, the theater sometimes upstages the performers, and the setting is certainly one reason families from all over the world have been coming here for more than 60 years. Many visit even when there are no concerts or events.

HEY, KIDS! Visit Red Rocks on a nonevent day or well before show time to test the amazing acoustics. Call to each other from different spots (including the stage, if there's access). It's said you can hear a whisper from stage even in some higher rows.

KEEP IN MIND Red Rocks has strict policies regarding what you can bring into the theater. Expect packs—even the kids'—to be checked at the gates. Allowed: coolers 12"×17" or smaller, binoculars, food (presliced), seat cushions, soft bags and packs, small umbrellas. Not allowed: unsealed plastic containers (even water bottles), thermoses, glass bottles, aluminum cans, knives or any potential weapon, noisemakers, laser pointers, recording devices, framed backpacks, skates, skateboards, animals, alcohol, any personal property potentially hazardous to others (according to official literature, "i.e., hula hoops"). Beer and wine are sold at concessions (I.D. is mandatory).

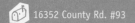
16352 County Rd. #93

Film series, $5–$8;
concert tickets vary

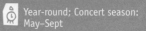
Year-round; Concert season:
May–Sept

303/295–4444;
www.redrocksonline.com

All ages

Which is not to downplay the artists. Red Rocks draws the world's musical greats—from rock legends to classical virtuosos—for the stunning acoustics alone. Though it's best known for rock concerts that parents and older teens can enjoy, the amphitheater hosts many family-friendly events. The summer movie series features classics and video staples such as *Independence Day* and *Forrest Gump*. As further enticement to go all the way to Red Rocks for a movie, the series includes musical performances. In the 2001 series, for example, the Colorado Symphony Orchestra played at the *Citizen Kane* showing, while the Denver Brass & Bagpipes appeared with *Braveheart*. Late each summer Reggae on the Rocks, one of the few daytime events, draws families with kids of all ages. And throughout the season there are folk, jazz, country, and blues concerts that multiple generations can enjoy together. As of September 2002, check out the new visitor center, with interactive kids' exhibits and information on local geology and musical history.

EATS FOR KIDS One of the best things about Red Rocks is having a picnic dinner or tailgate party. Join the friendly preshow crowds in the parking lots (no open-flame fires or charcoal grills allowed), or wait to dig into your picnic cooler when the show is underway, which can help break up the time for younger kids who may get antsy sitting through several hours of a performance. Pay attention to what you can and can't bring if you're going to picnic in the amphitheater (*see* Keep in Mind). Concessions have sandwiches, pizza, hot dogs, etc. ($2.50–$5.75).

ROCKY MOUNTAIN NATIONAL PARK

This is quintessential Rocky Mountain high country—lush valleys, flower-filled meadows, tundra, rushing streams, stunning peaks, aspen and fir forests, still lakes, and wild, rugged backcountry. It's all here in the 415 square miles of Rocky Mountain National Park (RMNP), a mere 75 miles from Denver. Superlatives abound. More than 60 mountains rise above 12,000 feet, with the tallest, Longs Peak, at 14,255 feet. The Continental Divide runs through the park, and Trail Ridge Road is the highest continuously paved highway in the United States—12,183 feet at its highest point. At its completion in 1932, Trail Ridge was heralded by the *Rocky Mountain News* as the "scenic wonder road of the world." Families should explore it not only for the stunning vistas—there are many—but for sightings of bighorn sheep and elk, all of which you can take in from the comfort of your car.

Trail Ridge isn't the only way to experience the park, and it would be a pity to come here and not get out on the trails. There are choices for all ages and abilities, so you're likely

HEY, KIDS! Become a Junior Ranger and get a badge. First, pick up a Junior Ranger Log Book at a visitor center. Next, read and sign the pledge promising to protect the environment. Then complete the activities, such as picking up litter in the park and attending a ranger-led program—not a problem because they're fun. There are morning, afternoon, and evening programs in different areas, so check with your parents to see which is best. Finally, be sure to give out Wildlife Guard stickers to other park visitors and explain why feeding wildlife is harmful. Way to go!

Estes Park

 970/586–1206; www.nps.gov; for reservations, reservations.nps.gov

 $15 per vehicle, $5 per adult arriving by foot, bicycle, horse, or motorcycle, ages 16 and under free. Camping fees extra.

 Beaver Meadows and Fall River visitor centers daily 9–5:30, Kawuneeche Visitor Center daily 8–4:30

All ages

to find one that's right for your crew. The walkways around the Beaver Ponds are easy even for very young children, and there's a ¾ mile (round-trip) nature trail from the Moraine Park Museum (check out the natural history exhibits first). The ½-mile Sprague Lake Trail has one of the best views of the Divide, and the 4-mile Gem Lake trail is studded with boulders perfect for kids who like to climb. More ambitious families can try the 2.7-mile hike (one way) to Ouzel Falls. They'll be rewarded with close-up views of daring ouzel birds plunging into rushing water. There are many possibilities, so your first stop should be a visitor center to get park and trail information and guides. RMNP is a place where families can experience nature at its most glorious while learning firsthand why our country's park system is a national treasure.

EATS FOR KIDS
The Trail Ridge Store at the Alpine Visitor Center has snacks, chili, sandwiches ($1–$4.95), and an observation deck. Or picnic at great sites off Bear Lake Rd., in Moraine Park, and at Lake Irene, among others. Estes Park and Grand Lake have grocery stores.

KEEP IN MIND The Rocky Mountain Nature Society runs terrific youth seminars in the park. Some are series (great for local kids) and others are one-time classes, such as nature photography for teens. Typically there are classes on such diverse subjects as nature sketchbooks, Native American leather and beads, and herbivores, carnivores, and omnivores. Rocky Mountain Nature Association is a nonprofit group whose mission is to offer participants expert insights into the park's rich natural and cultural heritage. Call 970/586–3262 or 800/748–7002 for more information.

SCOTT CARPENTER PARK

Proclaimed a park in 1955 and named after astronaut and one-time Boulder resident Scott Carpenter, this 21-acre city park has a little of everything—open grassy areas, playground, sun shelter, picnic facilities, ball field, swimming pool, and skatepark. Its space-theme playground, particularly the rocket slide, is a hit with young children, and in winter families congregate at the wide, gentle sledding hill. But the two biggest attractions are the outdoor pool and the skatepark.

The pool usually opens around Memorial Day and closes at the end of August. Kids and families can swim during open swim hours, and families with babies have their own baby pool hours as well. One corner of the lap pool is also set aside from 11 to 1 weekdays for parents who want to swim with their children under age five. One adult can supervise no more than three kids, and they must be no more than an arm's length away at all

EATS FOR KIDS The closest family restaurant is **Jose Muldoon's** (1600 38th St., tel. 303/449–4543) just down Arapahoe. The kids' menu has hamburgers and "donkey tails" (hot dogs in flour tortillas) and Mexican dishes ($2.25–$3.99); kids love the sopaipillas (75¢). Kids eat free Sunday nights.

KEEP IN MIND The skatepark is unsupervised—and also almost always crowded with fast-moving skaters and riders. If your kids are younger, bring them for Little Dude hours, 3:30–5 Wednesday and 10–11 Saturday. If your kids are older and you're not going to be staying to watch, let them know what to do in case of emergency. There's a public phone at the pool bathhouse, across the parking lot. Kids should know that they can call 911 at no charge, and that they should tell emergency operators where they are: Scott Carpenter Park at 30th and Arapahoe in Boulder.

times. The popular slide is open during open-swim times. Bring towels, and if you want to sit, bring your own pool chairs as well. Although this is an outdoor city pool, it's clean and well maintained, and a favorite of local families.

After much city controversy over the setting and planning, the skateboard park here was finally built in 2000, to the delight of area skateboarders and inline skaters—some of whom helped the architects with design details. In skatepark lingo this is a "street course" with rails and curbs to jump and ride and free-flowing forms and bowls, some of them steep enough to provide the kinds of thrills teens like, others a bit gentler for less experienced skaters and riders. The facility is open to BMX bikers every morning from 7 to 10. In an effort to deter graffiti elsewhere, artists are invited to be creative on the graffiti wall just north of the skatepark.

HEY, KIDS! Are you a skateboarder or inline skater? Check out the cool skatepark and challenge yourself—but do it safely. Always wear helmets and other protective gear, and follow park rules: no food or drink on riding surfaces, no glass, no pets or nonskating friends on the course. Before starting, make sure there's no trash or debris on the course—even little stuff can cause major wrecks. Don't skate or ride when the surface is wet (it's way dangerous), and, sorry, you can't add your own jumps or obstacles.

SIX FLAGS ELITCH GARDENS

Families have been playing at Elitch Gardens for more than a century. Elitch's, as everyone still calls it, moved to its present location in 1995 and was purchased by Six Flags in 1997. Today, the popular amusement park spans 60 acres close to downtown and offers more than 45 rides, shows, and attractions, including Island Kingdom Water Park (a park within the park).

Elitch's is a great choice for families with teens and preteens, a group generally in love with all that's fast and frightening. Point them to The Mind Eraser, a coaster that whips riders—with legs and feet dangling free—through rollovers, dives, and wicked corkscrew turns. Or maybe the 200-foot free-fall of Tower of Doom will be a perfect antidote to the adolescent "I'm bored" blues. It's not all for older kids, though. Looney Tunes MovieTown, for children under 54" tall, has 13 minirides, including a coaster. Over in the water park,

EATS FOR KIDS You can't bring food into Elitch's, but the park has typical fare from snack bars to full-service restaurants—all moderately priced. **Boardwalk Food Court,** by Shipwreck Falls, offers the largest variety; the quasi-'50s **Hollywood Diner,** near Mind Eraser, has burgers and shakes. **Rockin' E Buckaroo BBQ & Grill** is air-conditioned and centrally located. Or, after you leave Elitch's, try **PF Chang's** (1415 15th St., tel. 303/260–7222) in Denver's LoDo, where the Chinese food is delicious and anything but typical. No kids' menu, but few can resist crispy honey chicken, and shrimp dumplings are a must (about $7–$14).

 I–25 and Speer Blvd.,
Central Platte Valley

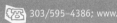 303/595-4386; www.sixflags.com

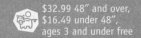 $32.99 48″ and over,
$16.49 under 48″,
ages 3 and under free

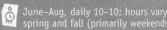 June–Aug, daily 10–10; hours vary
spring and fall (primarily weekends)

 All ages

Hook's Lagoon, with its five-story tree house and 150 water gadgets, is also for the small set. And there's everything else you'd want from an amusement park—a carousel, a Ferris wheel, super steel and wooden coasters, aqua slides, and raft rides.

No question this isn't a cheap day, but it's pretty much guaranteed fun. If you have kids of different ages (thus candidates for different rides and areas of the park), you may find need to split up, one adult going with older kids, another with younger. If you're planning to do both theme park and water park (no extra charge), have the kids wear swim suits under their clothes. Go on the dry rides first, then head to Island Kingdom to cool off. The theme park has a couple of water rides of its own that can soak you, especially Disaster Canyon, so you might want to save them until just before you go to Island Kingdom.

HEY, KIDS! Help your parents. Pick a place to meet in case anyone gets lost— say the base of the observation tower, because it's easy to spot. If you're lost, go there and wait. You can also go to a store and ask an employee for help.

KEEP IN MIND All of the rides have height restrictions. In some cases, children under a certain height can't ride at all, in others kids must be accompanied by an adult in order to ride. Measure your children before arriving at the park, then pick up the park map and guide when you enter. It lists all of the rides and height requirements and has lots of other useful information, such as locations for all guest services, including first aid, ATMs, restaurants and snacks, lockers, and shops. Give each child a park map, too, and circle the observation tower (see Hey, Kids!).

SIXTEENTH STREET MALL

9

This pedestrian mall, built in 1982, changed downtown from a place where few people went on evenings and weekends to a vibrant neighborhood with something fun to do day and night—all with the awesome backdrop of the Rocky Mountains. The mile-long mall is lined with 200 trees and dozens of flower-filled planters, along with fountains, plazas, and little "parkscapes" that make the heart of Denver a pleasant place to sit, stroll, and people-watch. Traffic is banned except for free shuttle buses that leave from either end of the mall every few minutes.

Many of the attractions in this book with the "Downtown" neighborhood designation are within walking distance of the mall; chances are if you're going to those places you'll pass by here. There's every reason to make this a principal destination, too. One of the big attractions for older kids is Denver Pavilions, a two-square-block entertainment complex that includes Nike Town, a Virgin Records Megastore, a state-of-the-art 15-

KEEP IN MIND For a complete listing of all of the events and festivals in Denver, including children's events, go to www.denvergov.org. Click on the searchable calendar for particular dates, or just run through the extensive listings and make plans to go downtown when there's something you want to see or do.

HEY, KIDS! If you think art is always in a museum or park, think again. Next time you're at the 16th Street Mall, go down Curtis Street between 15th and 16th and make a point to walk on the sidewalk grates. Why? Because as you do you might hear horses neighing, pigs grunting, trains whistling, toilets flushing, or birds chirping. The "talking" grates are one artist's idea of public art and a cool way to amuse friends or relatives who aren't expecting strange underground noises. The sounds change periodically, so check back every so often.

16th St. between Market and Broadway, Downtown

Free

303/892–1112 Denver Conventions & Visitors Bureau; www.denver.org

All day and evening hours

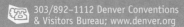
All ages

screen theater (including the 62-by-25-foot Big Screen), and more than 40 other shops and restaurants.

The mall is the setting for events and annual festivals, too, like the International BuskerFest, usually held in June, at which street performers from around the world congregate to juggle, perform magic, swallow swords, sing, tell jokes, and pass the hat. Each spring the Denver Public Schools Shakespeare Festival presents local school kids in works by the Bard. On Friday nights in summer drop in on free rock and R&B concerts. For 21 days in December, Christkindlmarket, a traditional German Christmas market (staffed by visiting Germans) features nutcrackers, blown-glass ornaments, gingerbread, and entertainment. In 2001 the American Skating Association set up a half-pipe on the mall where top skateboarders performed and local kids got to try their skills. On average, there's an event a week, so there's bound to be something families will want to see or do.

EATS FOR KIDS   There's no shortage of eateries on the mall: **Hard Rock Cafe** (*see #40*), **Maggiano's** (*see #40*), **Café Odyssey** (*see #49*), and **Wolfgang Puck's** are all excellent choices. Also popular is the **Cheesecake Factory** (1201 16th St., tel. 303/595–0333). The menu of this chain restaurant is as thick as a book (there are dozens of cheesecake flavors alone). Those who want their plates piled high love it, those of the "waste not want not" view may be appalled by the overload. Still, if it can be cooked it's here, and that's a plus for families with picky eaters ($6–$25).

SKI TRAIN

8

If you're heading for the mountains, why hassle with weekend traffic and being cooped up in a car? Instead you can have an adventure on the Ski Train, a Denver tradition since 1940. It's the perfect mode of transportation if you have both skiers (or boarders) and nonskiers in your group, because the trip itself is a minivacation—especially for train-loving kids.

The train departs historic Union Station for Winter Park (see #1) at 7:15 in the morning (8 in summer), taking a 56-mile route along the Flatirons and through South Boulder Canyon, past the towns of Pinecliffe and Rollinsville. (The return train leaves Winter Park at 4:15, 2:30 in summer.) It climbs some 4,000 feet and passes through 29 tunnels (let the kids count just to be sure), including the famous Moffat Tunnel, which burrows right under the Continental Divide. About two hours after leaving Denver, it stops less than 100 yards from the base of the chair lifts at Winter Park Resort. What could be

HEY, KIDS! Don't try holding your breath through the Moffat Tunnel, it's 6.2 miles long—the sixth longest tunnel in the world! And it's the highest railroad tunnel in the United States, 9,239 feet above sea level at the highest point. Building it was a long, hard job. During construction 750,000 cubic yards of rock were removed using 2.5 million pounds of dynamite. Each day 1,500 drills had to be sharpened. At a rate of about 21 feet per day, it took 48 months to finish the tunnel. The first train rolled through in 1928.

 Union Station, LoDo

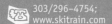 303/296-4754;
www.skitrain.com

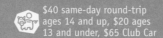 $40 same-day round-trip
ages 14 and up, $20 ages
13 and under, $65 Club Car

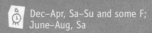 Dec–Apr, Sa–Su and some F;
June–Aug, Sa

 All ages

easier? On the way you can chat, relax, even snooze—or get together with your kids and read the souvenir "Ride Guide," so you can follow your path on the long and the winding track.

There's enough stunning scenery to make the early morning rise worthwhile; in fact, much of the scenery you can't see any other way. Plus, you get help with whatever equipment you bring along. In winter, folks at Union Station and on the train will assist you in loading your skis and boards. Go in summer and bring your mountain bikes—no bike rack required—so you and the kids can take to the many trails around Winter Park. Your trip can be as luxurious or casual as you like; the train has both coach and club car seating, as well as three luxury cars.

EATS FOR KIDS
There's food and beverage service throughout the train, and there are two café/lounge cars. Club car fares include Continental breakfast and apres-ski snacks. But it's also fun to do as those train-loving Europeans do: bring your own fruit, pastries, cheese, sandwiches, juice, and wine.

KEEP IN MIND Parking can be a challenge on a busy morning at Union Station, so plan on getting there early. It's a long way to run if you're late—the train's 17 cars stretch out over a quarter-mile! Advance ticket purchase is highly recommended. There are some added-value goodies that go with traveling via the Ski Train: in winter you can get discounted ski tickets, and in summer all fares include a coupon for one of the activities up at Winter Park, such as the alpine slide, chairlift ride, or mini-golf.

TATTERED COVER BOOKSTORE

7

Once there was a small bookstore beloved by its customers. Over time, it grew into a large bookstore known across the land. It has been called, more than once, the best bookstore in the country. Here's why.

To start, there's the cozy, welcoming feeling. Antique overstuffed chairs and sofas bathed in the warm light of reading lamps beckon you to curl up with a good book. The staff encourages adults and children to browse as long as they like, whether or not they buy a book. But you won't have trouble stocking the family bookshelf here. Between its two stores, Tattered Cover has more than a half-million books and 150,000 titles. The staff is extremely knowledgeable and service-oriented—they can tell you about more than what's on the best-seller lists. If it's in print, they'll find it for you, order it, and ship it if you like. If it's a gift, they'll wrap it for free.

EATS FOR KIDS In Cherry Creek, **Pasta, Pasta, Pasta** (278 Fillmore, tel. 303/377–2782) sells pasta dishes by the pound; open for lunch only ($5–$10). From the LoDo location, try **Dixon's Downtown Grill** (see #53) or **PF Chang's** (see #10).

HEY, KIDS! Log onto Tattered Cover's Web site, then click on Kids and Teens to see what's new and what events are coming up. If you're a creative type, watch for info on annual poetry and bookmark contests. Check out Kids' Links. Click on one of the titles and you'll be transported through cyberspace to publisher and author sites. On the Harry Potter site, for example, you can find such interesting things as a pronunciation guide. So how do you pronounce *Slytherin*, anyway?

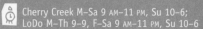

2955 E. 1st Ave., Cherry Creek;
1628 16th St., LoDo

303/322-7727 (Cherry Creek),
303/436-1070 (LoDo);
www.tatteredcover.com

 Free

Cherry Creek M–Sa 9 AM–11 PM, Su 10–6;
LoDo M–Th 9–9, F–Sa 9 AM–11 PM, Su 10–6

All ages

The children's section is a delight—expansive and stocked with all the popular titles, and lesser-known gems, too. If kids aren't sure what they want, a staff member will come up with stack of great suggestions to peruse. The downside is that kids never want to leave. Both stores have frequent story hours and author readings for kids—usually Saturdays at Cherry Creek, Thursdays at LoDo. The classic film series at LoDo is often a good bet for teens, too. The Cherry Creek store is a little bigger—four stories of books to LoDo's three— but LoDo has fireplaces to read by. And both locations have long-established coffee shops. Bottom line: Tattered Cover is a place for families to read, browse, shop, relax, listen to stories, meet cool authors, and indulge in the lap of literary luxury. It's one of Denver's true treasures.

KEEP IN MIND Hey parents! You should visit the Web site, too. You can buy books and gift certificates, subscribe to the store's newsletter— there's a section on kids' books—and get lots of information. At the Kids and Teens area, check out the suggested reading lists, for ages 3–6, 6–9, 10 and up, and 12 and up. There's even one for little ones from three months to three years. The Web site also highlights special events, such as Kids' Fair, which in years past has included stories, games, and, naturally, a Captain Underpants Giant Underpants Race.

TINY TOWN

In 1915 George Turner began erecting ⅙-scale turn-of-the-20th-century buildings to amuse his daughter. The collection opened to the public in 1920, and though it was a two- to three-hour drive over bone-jarring dirt roads from Denver, Tiny Town was a success. By 1939 it was declared "world famous" and featured a small working railroad.

Whether or not Tiny Town was ever really known worldwide, it's been much loved by locals for nearly a century—although floods, fires, and financial problems have threatened it and sent it into decline several times through the years. Its special place in the hearts of Colorado families was demonstrated in the late 1980s, when volunteers from throughout the state refurbished it, adding new buildings and getting the railroad up and running again. Today, Tiny Town has more than 100 colorful buildings and, through the miracle of modern transportation, is just 30 minutes from downtown Denver.

HEY, KIDS! Tiny Town is a nonprofit institution, which means that it only keeps part of the money it makes each year—just enough to pay for upkeep and expenses, including the salaries of the people who work there. The rest of the money goes to local charities. You can help, too. While you're there, make sure you stop by the wishing well. Any coins you drop in will be donated to a Denver-area children's hospital to help sick children and their families. And you might just get a wish fulfilled in the bargain.

6249 S. Turkey Creek Rd.; off US–285

303/697–6829;
www.designcircuit.com/eic/tiny.htm
l

 $3 ages 13 and up,
$2 ages 3–12, under 3
free; train fare $1

June–Aug, daily 10–5; May, Sept–Oct,
Sa–Su 10–5

All ages

Tiny Town's own downtown includes a fire station, toy store, ice cream shop, theater, gas station, school, and library. Out in the residential area are houses, mansions, and several churches. There's even a radio station. It's hard to say why exactly this miniature village holds such appeal, but being there brings a smile to your face. Some families like the train best; adults and kids ride open cars pulled by a steam engine on the 1-mile loop through town and into the canyon, getting an overview of the place before they explore on foot. Others enjoy peering into tiny windows at the elaborately decorated interiors of some buildings. And a favorite for many kids is crawling through the few buildings set up for that. As one little girl put it, "It's like being in that scene from *Alice in Wonderland*, you know, the one when she took the pill that made her really, really big." That's a very apt comparison.

EATS FOR KIDS
In nearby Morrison is the **Morrison Inn** (see #34) with its moderately priced Mexican food. If it's dinnertime, consider **The Fort** (see #29) for exotic, though expensive, Western fare.

GETTING HERE Tiny Town is not near anything to speak of. The easiest way to reach it from Denver is via C–470 from I–25 (C–470 loops around so there are exits for it off I–25 both north and south of downtown). Exit at US 285, go west for 5 miles, then turn left on South Turkey Creek Road by the Tiny Town sign (which is fairly tiny itself). If you're coming from the Littleton vicinity, you can also take US 285 directly (or from I–25), turning onto South Turkey Creek Road 5 miles past the C–470/US 285 interchange.

UNITED STATES MINT

In the 1800s and early 1900s, Colorado produced a rash of folks who were suddenly rich from digging gold and silver out of the hills. They needed a coinage facility for all that precious metal, and the solution to their enviable problem was Denver's mint. The mint today is no less essential, and not just for mining millionaires. The Denver facility manufactures 40 million coins a day—that's 8 billion a year. Why do we need so many coins? It seems Americans lose or stash $100,000 in pennies each and every day, and it's the job of the U.S. Mint to replace them.

Approximately 70 percent of the coins stamped in Denver are pennies. You can witness this massive—and noisy—process on a tour that gives you a clear view of dozens of humongous presses spitting out as many as 800 coins a minute into big piles. What happens to those piles? You find out in another viewing area where you watch coins counted,

EATS FOR KIDS Racine's (850 Bannock, tel. 303/595–0418) offers breakfast, lunch, and dinner in a laid-back atmosphere. The varied menu is good, and the brownies are renowned—the Secretary of Energy had some flown to Washington. There's a typical kids' menu ($3.50 with drink and ice cream).

HEY, KIDS! After the tour you can stop at a minipress and get your own coin stamped (there's a small fee) to take away as a souvenir. And if the tour gets you interested in coins and collecting, be sure to log onto the U.S. Mint Web site. You'll find lots of fascinating information, including how to get started collecting coins. There are also games, mysteries, and other fun stuff. Just click on "h.i.p. pocket change" to get to the kids' area.

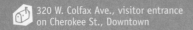 320 W. Colfax Ave., visitor entrance
on Cherokee St., Downtown

 Free, but tickets
are required

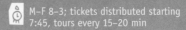 M–F 8–3; tickets distributed starting
7:45, tours every 15–20 min

 303/405-4761 or 303/405-4765;
www.usmint.gov

 5 and up

sorted, and bagged. The tour starts with a bit of history and education about the process of stamping coins, and ends in the Numismatic Sales Room, where collectors of all ages can purchase commemorative and other collectable coins. Older kids and adults will find the information provided on the relatively short tour (about 15 minutes) interesting. For most children, though, it's the site of all those piles of coins, as well as six 27-pound gold bars, that's most memorable. What you don't see is even more impressive—about $100 billion worth of gold bars secured in the basement! Denver is second only to Fort Knox as a gold repository.

Because seeing the machines spitting out zillion of coins is really the highlight, check ahead to make sure that production is in full swing. Although tours are offered year-round, production usually shuts down around the last week of June and first week of July.

KEEP IN MIND June through September is the busiest season for tours at the U.S. Mint, and more visitors show up than can be accommodated. Sometimes the line is cut off as early as noon in order to ensure that everyone who waits can enter the tour area by 2:45. Worse, the average wait in line can easily be an hour, a challenge for even the most enthusiastic kids. If you're planning to tour during this time period, make the Mint your first activity of the day so you and the kids aren't disappointed.

USGS NATIONAL EARTHQUAKE
INFORMATION CENTER

4

The U.S. Geological Survey (USGS) runs the National Earthquake Information Center (NEIC), a 24/7 earthquake alert system. The job of scientists here is to determine quickly and accurately the location and magnitude of significant earthquakes throughout the world, then get that information to local experts, emergency management teams, and public safety agencies. (Railroads, power plants, and pipeline companies are alerted as well.) Also, seismologists around the world use NEIC's data to better understand earthquakes and more effectively evaluate earthquake hazards.

If this all sounds high tech and complex, it is: approximately 3,000 regional seismic stations report to the NEIC, and at the facility state-of-the-art equipment abounds. Yet this is a place where all kinds of visitors, including children, are welcome. If you're under the impression that geology is a yawn, the 30- to 45-minute tour could change your mind. In fact, it's less of a tour than an Earthquake 101 overview—and you and the kids will be anything

HEY, KIDS! In the past 100 years, where in the world were the largest earthquakes, and how big were they? According to NEIC, these were the locations of the top 10 (starting with the largest): Chile (1960); Prince William Sound, Alaska (1964); Aleutian Islands (1957); Kamchatka (in the Bering Sea, 1952); off the coast of Ecuador (1906); Aleutian Islands (1965); India–China Border (1950); Kamchatka (1923); Banda Sea, Indonesia (1938); Kuril Islands, Japan (1963). They ranged in magnitude from 9.5 to 8.5. Check a map; see any patterns? Are there any similarities between these places?

1711 Illinois St., 5th Floor, Room 530, Golden

Free

By appointment, T–Th, 9 AM–11 AM, 1 PM–3 PM

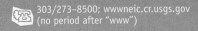303/273–8500; wwwneic.cr.usgs.gov (no period after "www")

10 and up

but bored. You'll see the earthquake monitoring room and learn not only about what NEIC and its affiliates around the world do—fascinating from a technology standpoint alone—but also about what causes earthquakes, how they are measured, what faults are, and more. A lot of what you get from the experience depends on the questions you ask (you'll have plenty of opportunity); children's questions are answered with the same respect and interest as those from adults.

If Waverly Person, Chief of the National Earthquake Information Service, is your guide, make a point to remember his face. You're likely to see it on the news the next time a major earthquake hits somewhere in the world, because he's an expert that newscasters frequently turn to. Before leaving, stop at the display on the first floor where you can jump up and down and watch the seismometer measure your own "earthquakes."

KEEP IN MIND
Call well ahead to get your choice of tours, and allow time to park and get up to the center. Parking is available behind the building, on the street, or in the Colorado School of Mines free lot, southwest corner of 18th and Illinois.

EATS FOR KIDS Table Mountain Inn (1310 Washington Ave., Golden, tel. 303/277–9898) is southwestern with a flare. Kids might go for many of the items on the regular menu, but they can opt for penne, quesadillas, chicken strips, or burgers—all served with choice of fruit, fries, or cole slaw—from the children's menu ($3.95 with drink). As for parents, there's a varied luncheon menu including southwestern dishes such as chili rellenos, chicken, and lots more ($5.95–$9.95). If you're in the area for dinner, it's also a real treat.

WASHINGTON PARK

The 165-acre "Wash Park" is one of Denver's most popular city parks, and its rec center one of the busiest. It has just about everything you'd hope for in an urban park—and then some. Whether you and the kids want to bike, walk, jog, run, swim, fish, or play a variety of sports, you can do it here. The park's gardens are among the most beautiful and largest in the city park system, and from spring to the first autumn frost masses of blooms brighten lawns and pathways. The designs change every year, providing surprises from one season to the next. One of the gardens, created in 1926, is a replica of Martha Washington's garden at Mount Vernon in Virginia.

Washington Park reflects the spirit of Denver's active, outdoor-loving citizens. On any given sunny afternoon (and there are more than 300 of them annually) you'll find people of all ages around the park using the sports facilities. There are soccer fields and tennis courts, a crushed-granite jogging path, a bicycle–pedestrian pathway, and places to

KEEP IN MIND

Although cyclists and skaters are discouraged from going too fast on park paths, the reality is that many whoosh by at frightening speeds—frightening especially to youngsters and beginners on wheels. Warn kids in advance and encourage them to stay in one lane.

EATS FOR KIDS

There are lots of restaurants on South Gaylord, but they're aimed more at the area yuppie types than kids. Still, you'll find plenty of families at **Washington Park Grille** (1096 S. Gaylord, tel. 303/777–0707), which features Italian and American cuisine. The kids' menu has burgers, pizza, and macaroni and cheese entrées ($3.50, including drink and ice cream). For adults there are sandwiches, pastas, and more ($8–$15 lunch, $12–$22 dinner). For a real treat, join the throngs of families from the park indulging in homemade ice cream at **Bonnie Brae** (799 S. University, tel. 303/777–0808).

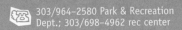
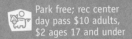
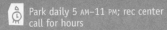

play croquet, lawn bowling, and horseshoes. Two lakes, Smith in the north and Grasmere in the south, provide a place for shoreside anglers to test their skills against resident sunfish, trout, bass, and carp. (You must have a state license if you're over the age of 16.) Lily Pond is for kids' fishing only (ages 16 and under). Inline skaters love the blacktop roadway ringing the park, which is closed to traffic—a particular boon for families with skaters. And younger kids can be found whiling away the hours at either of two great playgrounds.

Do check out the rec center. It has drop-in classes, weight rooms, swimming, and more. Residents and nonresidents can purchase day passes. Sometimes the municipal band plays in the park; at www.denvergov.org/event you can find out what's happening in Washington Park and around the city.

HEY, KIDS! Hungry after all that running around in the park? If you're craving protein and want to order a cheeseburger in a nearby restaurant, there's something you should know: that all-American meal on a bun, the cheeseburger, was invented right here in Denver! It was back in 1935 at a Humpty Dumpty drive-in restaurant. Louis Ballast melted a slice of cheese on a hamburger, called it a cheeseburger, and voila! History was made. Just imagine what dinner in America would be like without Louis's innovation.

WINGS OVER THE ROCKIES AIR & SPACE MUSEUM

You have no idea just how huge the B-1 bomber is until you stand under one—and here's your chance. The B-1 and about 30 other military and civilian aircraft and space vehicles make up the heart of the collection at Wings Over the Rockies.

Everything is housed in a massive World War II–era hangar that kids can wander around in, being awed and more awed as they see what these flying machines are like up close. The museum also has exhibits of military uniforms, model planes, the home of President Eisenhower when he spent a summer at Lowry Airforce Base (Mamie Eisenhower was from Denver), and other historical artifacts. But what most visitors are really drawn to are the planes. There's a replica of a German glider used to train pilots for the Luftwaffe, an enormous B-52, and the H-21C helicopter, known by the nickname "the Giant Flying Banana," and with good reason. There are planes built in the 1920s and from the era of the Strategic Air Command (1946–92), rare machines and classics, too, some on the ground and some hanging from the ceiling.

KEEP IN MIND Although preschoolers love looking at airplanes—and get something at their own level out of the experience—the museum and its education programs target ages eight and older. For example, the on-site Fantasy of Flight Education Center runs programs throughout the year during which kids make Styrofoam model planes and experience flight simulators. On Open Cockpit Days (second Saturday of every other month beginning in January), kids can actually go into two or three of the exhibit cockpits and talk to pilots on hand who provide information and answer questions. These talks are too sophisticated for very young children.

7711 East Academy Blvd., East Denver

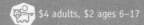 $4 adults, $2 ages 6–17

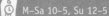 M–Sa 10–5, Su 12–5

303/360-5360;
www.wingsovertherockies.org

 3 and up

This airplane-lover's paradise is dedicated to preserving historic air and space vehicles and also the history of the men and women who flew them. Colorado has its share of famous aviators, including astronaut Scott Carpenter (*see #11* for the Boulder park named after him). The Denver area also has a rich aviation history. The museum is on the former site of the Lowry Airforce Base, which closed in 1994 when the military made cutbacks. You can't climb in or on the displays—the space station model is an exception—but most kids are enthralled just by the sight of the machinery. If the real planes don't impress them, there's always Luke Skywalker's famous X-Wing fighter from the Star Wars movies—and what kid wouldn't be impressed with that?

EATS FOR KIDS

Head back toward downtown via Colfax and stop at **Good-friends** (3100 E. Colfax, tel. 303/399–1751), where kids can choose from ziti with white or red sauce, burritos, grilled cheese, and more ($2.95), while adult choices include southwestern fare, ahi tuna, fried chicken, steak, and salads.

HEY, KIDS! You'll know you're at the right place when you see the *humongous* B-52 *Stratofortress* parked outside the hangar. This is one big plane. Here are the stats: it's over 159 feet long, more than 40 feet high, and it has a wingspan of 185 feet. (To compare, the Statue of Liberty is just over 150 feet tall from base to top of torch.) The B-52 weighs 185,000 pounds empty and can fly nearly 9,000 miles before having to refuel. It flies up to 650 miles per hour and as high as 50,000 feet in the air.

WINTER PARK RESORT

Denver is blessed with 47 mountain parks—territories beyond the city's borders that between them preserve every type of landscape and habitat found in Colorado, from flat prairie to alpine tundra. The most famous of these is Winter Park Resort, a favorite front-range summer playground and world-class winter ski area. Coming from the city you climb more than 3,700 feet to reach the base, winding over Berthoud Pass by car or through 29 tunnels by train (see #8). Once you've arrived, the object is to play.

In winter, families can ski or board on 134 downhill trails, go snowshoeing and cross-country skiing through pristine Rocky Mountain winterscapes, take sleigh rides and snowcat tours, or even try dogsledding. There's also ice skating, and visitors and locals alike can be found whooping it up in nearby Frasier on the famous tubing hill—yep, whooshing downhill on big, old-fashioned inner tubes. Winter Park has an excellent children's ski

KEEP IN MIND Avoid altitude sickness—headaches, nausea, or more severe symptoms—by drinking lots of water, even if you're not thirsty. Remind kids to drink, too, and don't overdo exercise upon first arrival. Some folks swear that reducing protein and increasing carbs also prevents altitude illness.

HEY, KIDS! Snowboarding originated in the 1970s when a surfer designed a "snurfer" so he could surf on snow (think two skis bolted together). Another snurfer found a way to improve the design, and the first real snowboards appeared. Although some encyclopedias have insisted on listing snowboarding under skiing, it's really closer to surfing or skateboarding in its movements and rhythm—and in its attitude. Snowboarding is the fastest growing winter sport today. When you try it, keep this in mind: if your stance is too wide you can't turn; if it's too narrow you won't have good balance.

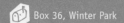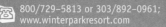

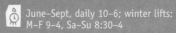

Box 36, Winter Park

800/729-5813 or 303/892-0961;
www.winterparkresort.com

Summer activity
tickets $6–$45;
winter lift tickets
$15–$35

June–Sept, daily 10–6; winter lifts:
M–F 9–4, Sa–Su 8:30–4

3 and up

and snowboard school, so if your kids want to learn, this is a good place for it. And if you're thinking of trying to keep up with your kids on the slippery slopes, sign up for an adult lesson or two.

In summer, come here for fun in the mountain sunshine. Kids can challenge parents on the mountain-theme mini-golf course (those little tunnels are killers), and the whole family can ride the Zephyr Express chairlift up to 10,700 feet for awesome views and perhaps a hike or mountain-bike ride back down. Or ride the lift down and catch the views from another perspective. For family fun at slightly lower elevations, there's the rip-roaring alpine slide—choose the slow or fast lane. If you can make it through the human maze in record time, you might win a T-shirt. (Hint: plan on taking the challenge more than once!) Still not enough? Try the climbing wall at the base or go horseback riding nearby.

EATS FOR KIDS An outrageously unscientific survey has found, definitively, that the French fries at **Sunspot** (at the top of the Zephyr Express) are the best in the world. Decide for yourself at either of the two restaurants where choices include soups, salads, grilled sandwiches, burgers, chicken fingers, and more ($3.75–$11). Down at the base, **Kickipoo Tavern** has usual lunch fare and such dinner entrées as trout. The "Lil Opossum" menu offers kids chicken, dogs, pizza, and more ($5.95). Whatever you have, leave room for the peanut butter cake ($5).

extra! extra!

CLASSIC GAMES

"I SEE SOMETHING YOU DON'T SEE AND IT IS BLUE." Stuck for a way to get your youngsters to settle down in a museum? Sit them down on a bench in the middle of a room and play this vintage favorite. The leader gives just one clue—the color—and everybody guesses away.

"I'M GOING TO THE GROCERY..." The first player begins, "I'm going to the grocery and I'm going to buy... " and finishes the sentence with the name of an object, found in grocery stores, that begins with the letter "A." The second player repeats what the first player has said, and adds the name of another item that starts with "B." The third player repeats everything that has been said so far and adds something that begins with "C" and so on through the alphabet. Anyone who skips or misremembers an item is out (or decide up front that you'll give hints to all who need 'em). You can modify the theme depending on where you're going that day, as "I'm going to X and I'm going to see..."

FAMILY ARK Noah had his ark—here's your chance to build your own. It's easy: just start naming animals and work your way through the alphabet, from antelope to zebra.

PLAY WHILE YOU WAIT

NOT THE GOOFY GAME Have one child name a category. (Some ideas: first names, last names, animals, countries, friends, feelings, foods, hot or cold things, clothing.) Then take turns naming things that fall into that category. You're out if you name something that doesn't belong in the category—or if you can't think of another item to name. When only one person remains, start again. Choose categories depending on where you're going or where you've been—historic topics if you've seen a historic sight, animal topics before or after the zoo, upside-down things if you've been to the circus, and so on. Make the game harder by choosing category items in A-B-C order.

DRUTHERS How do your kids really feel about things? Just ask. "Would you rather eat worms or hamburgers? Hamburgers or candy?" Choose serious and silly topics—and have fun!

BUILD A STORY "Once upon a time there lived…" Finish the sentence and ask the rest of your family, one at a time, to add another sentence or two. Bring a tape recorder along to record the narrative—and you can enjoy your creation again and again.

GOOD TIMES GALORE

WIGGLE & GIGGLE Give your kids a chance to stick out their tongues at you. Start by making a face, then have the next person imitate you and add a gesture of his own—snapping fingers, winking, clapping, sneezing, or the like. The next person mimics the first two and adds a third gesture, and so on.

JUNIOR OPERA During a designated period of time, have your kids sing everything they want to say.

THE QUIET GAME Need a good giggle—or a moment of calm to figure out your route? The driver sets a time limit and everybody must be silent. The last person to make a sound wins.

HIGH FIVES

BEST IN TOWN
Brown Palace Afternoon Tea
Denver Art Museum
Denver Public Library
E-Town
Rocky Mountain National Park

BEST MUSEUM
Denver Museum of Nature and Science

BEST CULTURAL ACTIVITY
Central City Opera Youth Performance

BEST OUTDOORS
Winter Park

WACKIEST
Outdoor Film Festival

NEW & NOTEWORTHY
Renovations and expansions of Childrens's Museum of Denver,
Denver Art Museum, and Denver Museum of Nature & Science

SOMETHING FOR EVERYONE

ALL AROUND TOWN

MANY THANKS!

I t takes a village to raise a child—and a whole army to write a book! Because Denver is so activity oriented, culturally rich, and typically Western in how spread out it is, the research alone was a mind-boggling task. I never could have learned all I needed to learn without the indefatigable help of Karin Lazarus and Kathy Schenck. My thanks, too, to Liz Helmick, who happily did site research and got answers when I needed them at a moment's notice. My children Molly and Hutch and my niece Lucie managed not only good cheer and much needed energy, but also offered awesome "kid" insights crucial to the integrity of this book. I appreciate the efforts of all of the PR folks who provided me with information and answered endless questions, and a special thanks to Rich Grant of the Denver Convention and Visitors Bureau, whose particular humor and extensive knowledge have made him a valued colleague for many years. Thank you Doug Stahl for taking me out for excellent barbecue, and Kelly Greten for taking care of things when I was under deadline. Finally, my thanks to editor Matt Lombardi for his understanding and generosity of spirit under some difficult circumstances, and, of course, for his most excellent editing and direction.

—Christine Loomis

the end